Rethink...For a Change

Transformed Living through Transformed Thinking

Rick Roepke, D.Min

WESTBOW
PRESS®
A DIVISION OF THOMAS NELSON
& ZONDERVAN

This book is a work of non-fiction. Unless otherwise noted, the author and the publisher make no explicit guarantees as to the accuracy of the information contained in this book and in some cases, names of people and places have been altered to protect their privacy.

WestBow Press books may be ordered through booksellers or by contacting:

WestBow Press
A Division of Thomas Nelson & Zondervan
1663 Liberty Drive
Bloomington, IN 47403
www.westbowpress.com
1 (866) 928-1240

ISBN: 978-1-9736-7454-2 (sc)
ISBN: 978-1-9736-7455-9 (hc)
ISBN: 978-1-9736-7453-5 (e)

Library of Congress Control Number: 2019913756

Print information available on the last page.

WestBow Press rev. date: 10/28/2019

Contents

PART ONE
The Thought Process

PART TWO
Changing Your Life's Recipes

Acknowledgments

First, I want to thank my heavenly Father and my Lord and Savior Jesus Christ, the Author and perfecter of my faith, who died on the cross so that all who believe in Him may have eternal life.

To my beautiful wife Kathy, who not only is the love of my life but is also the biggest supporter of my dreams, I love you! And thank you to my children, Emily and Erik, who truly are blessings from God.

Two men, Jeff Reed and Greg Wood, have been a constant source of encouragement and sometimes the push that I needed to step out and do what God was calling me to do…big thanks to you!

And finally, my editor Vanessa Carroll, who is a godsend. Thank you so much for your incredible talents on this project.

Introduction

When my mom's family emigrated from Stockholm, Sweden, they brought several Scandinavian traditions with them. One of the traditions was Christmas Eve dinner. The main dish was called cabbage pudding. Before you start to wrinkle up your nose or gag at the thought of a pudding made from cabbage, it's not what you think. Cabbage pudding is a meat dish, like a layered meatloaf with all kinds of spices. It is wonderful!

My mom continued this Christmas Eve tradition with us when we were kids. I can remember the heavenly aroma of cabbage pudding filling the house until we could hardly stand it. We all hovered around her in the kitchen like baby birds, mouths open wide and drooling, all crying out to be fed first! She pretended to get mad at us, and I can still hear her saying in her thick Swedish accent: "Go on now and get out of the kitchen! Go do something! I can't turn for stepping on one of you! So, go on if you want me to finish!"

It's funny how we remember the small things when we look back, and these are the things we miss the most. Mom died in 1983 at the age of fifty-six after a long bout with liver cancer. When she died, a lot of our family traditions died with her. Three years ago, I decided to bring back the tradition of cabbage pudding and make it for my family for Christmas. I found the recipe card in some of my mom's old papers and was able to duplicate what my mom's family started so many years ago by following the recipe. I followed the steps on the recipe card, and I was able to recreate the dish. The flavors and smells brought me back to my childhood, and my family loved it. It was a success!

If I had changed the steps or ingredients, I would have changed the outcome of the recipe. What if instead of using cabbage, I grabbed a rotten zucchini from my refrigerator's vegetable drawer? I could have sliced it up thinly and made it look like cabbage, but we can imagine how that would taste, and we can envision my family's reactions: gagging, spitting, running to the bathroom . . . it would have been a failure. Cabbage pudding is the by-product of following the recipe. As long as I do what is written down, I will always end up with cabbage pudding. If I use bad ingredients, I will get a bad outcome. If I use good ingredients, I will get a good outcome.

That's how life can be as well. Our minds process through thousands of thought cycles every hour. Without knowing it, we are engaging in the thought process all day long. It starts with a circumstance or event, which triggers our thoughts. Our thoughts trigger our emotions. Our emotions dictate our behavior. Our behaviors bring about good or bad outcomes. Each of us has developed our own thought patterns over a lifetime. It's like developing and following our own recipe we've created.

We are always following a recipe. We are either following a recipe of our own creation or one passed down to us from previous generations. Some of our recipes are great! We feel good about them, and they are producing positive outcomes! In fact, we feel energized following these recipes! On the other hand, we follow some recipes that are not so good. These are the ones that keep us up at night, or wake us up at 1:00 a.m., stressed out about the issues we're facing, often to the point of getting physically ill.

We have both good and bad recipes in our life's recipe box. We follow certain steps, and we receive an outcome based on those steps. The more closely we follow the steps on the card, the more likely we are to receive the by-product of the recipe. Our successes, happy relationships, and inner peace—or our failures, difficult relationships, and inner angst—are all outcomes of the recipes we are following.

"The significant problems that we face cannot be solved at the same level of thinking that it took to create it in the first place."[1] In other words, if you keep on doing what you've always done, you will keep on getting what you've always gotten. There are a lot of folks who want a different life for themselves. They want to be happier, they want to be in a better relationship, they want to lose weight, or be more physically fit. Others want to be financially healthy by becoming debt free. Unfortunately, their actions don't reflect their wants. They keep on doing the same old thing, expecting things to be different. When it isn't any different, they become more and more frustrated, which can bring on feelings of hopelessness and wanting to totally give up.

We want something different in life. We are tired of the same old stuff that trips us up. However, we continue to use the same ingredients that caused us pain in the first place. We just don't learn, especially when we know what the bad ingredients are when we pick them up. Proverbs 26:11 says, "As a dog returns to its vomit, so fools repeat their folly." Not a pleasant picture when you think about it! But neither is what happens to us when we continue to repeat our harmful patterns.

Imagine one day you had a craving for brownies; however, all you could find was a recipe for goulash. So you, being the clever person you are, took the recipe card, marked out the word "goulash," and wrote "brownies" over it. You followed the steps on the recipe card, all the while expecting that in just a little bit, you

---

[1] http://www.quotationspage.com/quote/23588.html

would be munching on brownies. You told yourself, "They will be brownies." You envisioned yourself eating them with a cold glass of milk, and even imagined that you smelled them baking in the oven. But the reality was, because you did nothing to change the ingredients to align with your desired outcome, you disappointedly, and with major frustration, ended up with . . . goulash!

The same thing happens if I want a healthy, strong, and vibrant marriage. If all I do is relabel the "unhealthy marriage" recipe with "healthy marriage," still following the ingredients and instructions that produced the unhealthy relationship, I will still get an unhealthy marriage. No matter how badly I want a better marriage, the outcome will be the same.

Florence Scovel Shinn said, "If one asks for success and prepares for failure, he will get the situation he has prepared for."[2] I can want for something all day long, but if my actions don't reflect my wants, it won't happen. What we prepare for determines what happens to us.

This book will explore ways in which we contaminate our life's recipes—recipes for ourselves, our relationships, and our situations. We will identify contaminants, learn how to reduce or eliminate them, and replace them with contributing factors. In doing so, we will rewrite a healthy and balanced life recipe.

---

[2] http://thinkexist.com/quotation/if-one-asks-for-success-and-prepares-for-failure/761673.html

PART ONE
The Thought Process

"You were taught, with regard to your former way of life, to put off your old self, which is being corrupted by its deceitful desires; to be made new in the attitude of your minds; and to put on the new self, created to be like God in true righteousness and holiness."

Ephesians 4:22-24

"We design our lives through the power of choices."

Richard Bach

CHAPTER ONE

Stress

The seed that fell among the thorns represents those who hear God's word, but all too quickly the message is crowded out by the worries of this life and the lure of wealth, so no fruit is produced.

Matthew 13:22 NLT

It was a dark morning in Brooklyn, as dark as it could be at two in the morning. Jerry never slept a full night. He could never stop thinking long enough to rest. It was a common thing with Jerry, like a pattern. He laid on the ground, wide awake, heart pounding, thoughts racing, unable to relax. One more attempt at falling asleep was as useless as the next. Sleep just didn't fit into the agenda.

His thoughts recently had become increasingly negative. Jerry was becoming quite the pessimist. He worried all the time and could rarely focus on the task at hand. He had no more friends, no motivation, nothing but pent up anger and unhappiness.

With a great sigh and pain welling up in his chest, Jerry got to his feet and scurried down the steps to the kitchen.

"There is never anything to eat in this stupid house," he muttered to himself.

After a few moments of sifting through the pantry and draining the last few drops of alcohol, Jerry made his way back to the door. He was always hungry, and surely there were restaurants still open.

As he approached the door, he noticed a dark figure in the corner. Jerry's heart stopped. I can't believe he's still following me, he thought. His heart raced. He began to shake, and the room started to spin.

Without much thought, Jerry leapt behind the sofa. He sat as quietly as he could, trying to think, but he couldn't concentrate. He felt weak and irritable from lack of sleep. Anxiously, Jerry began to gnaw on his fingernails, biting each one until they were nearly too short. After what seemed like forever, Jerry slowly peeked his head around the edge of the sofa, looking for the figure who sat there night after night, lurking, hunting, waiting for him to take one wrong step.

If Jerry hadn't isolated himself from the rest of the family, he might not feel so alone right now. He had been unhappy with his life for a while now, and his parents were cracking down on his weight gain. His heart was about to pound its way out of his chest now as he took the first few steps to the back door. Jerry remained as quiet as a mouse as he tried to slink to the door. Then, still recovering from last week's cold, the urge to cough overwhelmed him. He tried to hold it in until he ran out of breath. Jerry coughed as silently as he could, but it was useless. The figure leapt from his corner and bounded toward Jerry.

Jerry squeaked as he bolted in the other direction, straight for the wall of the tiny New York apartment. He held his breath as he neared the wall and sped up with a burst of adrenaline, straight into the tiny hole in the baseboard. Once he was safe from harm, he laid down on the cold concrete, gasping for air. He was shaky, dizzy, nauseous, angry, and alone. Jerry was agitated and, once again, lifted his hand to bite at his nails.

Jerry thought of his wife and how unsatisfied she was with their love life. She couldn't handle his ever-changing moods, so he had run away. He should have never lost his temper with his family. Jerry could still be safe in his home if he'd had better judgment, but stress got the best of him. If he hadn't neglected his responsibilities, he would be surrounded by loved ones, not being chased by Tom, the cat. It is extremely stressful to be a rat in New York City. [3]

Poor Jerry! It must be hard to be a rat plagued by stress in the big city, or anywhere else for that matter. To be constantly on guard, always looking over your shoulder, being haunted by the "what ifs" and "should haves, could haves, would haves," and having a nagging sense of impending doom (when is the cat going to pounce?). We know this story about Jerry is fictitious, but what is not fictitious is that a lot of people in the world are experiencing the same things our little friend Jerry was experiencing. Here are some signs and symptoms that indicate you are living a stressed-out life like Jerry. See if you can relate to any of them.

Stress Warning Signs and Symptoms

Cognitive Symptoms

- Memory problems
- Inability to concentrate
- Poor judgment
- Seeing only the negative
- Anxious or racing thoughts
- Constant worry

---

[3] This story was written by my beautiful and incredibly creative daughter, Emily Roepke Rudolph.

Physical Symptoms

- Aches and pains
- Diarrhea or constipation
- Nausea
- Dizziness
- Chest pain
- Rapid heartbeat
- Loss of sex drive
- Frequent colds

Emotional Symptoms

- Moodiness
- Irritability or short temper
- Agitation, inability to relax
- Feeling overwhelmed
- Sense of loneliness and isolation
- Depression or general unhappiness

Behavioral Symptoms

- Eating more or eating less than normal
- Sleeping too much or too little
- Isolating yourself from others
- Procrastinating or neglecting responsibilities
- Using alcohol, cigarettes, or drugs to relax
- Nervous habits (nail biting, pacing, etc.)

All Stressed Up with No Place to Go

What Jerry and many people in our society are experiencing are symptoms caused by toxic stress. A hundred years ago, the major causes of death were farming accidents, childbirth with secondary infection, and pneumonia.[4] These things happened *to* us. These days, we are dying from "diseases of adaptation." When toxic stress is left unchecked, it can lead to such things as obesity, heart disease, high blood pressure, stroke, TMJ, irritable bowel syndrome, and the list goes on and on! We are doing this to ourselves. We are living such stressful lives we would make a Valium nervous.

A recent study stated that 90 percent of doctor visits and hospitalizations were either caused by or were complicated by stress.[5] Henry Kissinger sums it up nicely: "There cannot be a stressful crisis next week. My schedule is already full."

Life Is Driving Me Nuts (and It's a Short Trip)!

Our lives can be full of demands, deadlines, and frustrations. In fact, a little stress can be good for us. It can act as a motivator and enhance our performance. But when it continues, that which was designed to help us becomes toxic.

For some well-meaning, yet misguided people, toxic stress is such a way of life that they see it as a companion they've been hanging out with since birth. Their mantra is, "What does not kill me makes me stronger." Unfortunately, when it comes to living with high levels of stress, they are wrong. Not only does prolonged stress shorten life spans, it can also be a killer of relationships.

Let's go more deeply into the causes of stress and the effects it can have on your body, your mental health, and your life.

---

[4] CDC.gov
[5] HuffPost.com and the American Psychological Association

CHAPTER TWO

The Source of Stress

Each choice we make causes a ripple effect in our lives.
When things happen to us, it is the reaction we choose
that can create the difference between the sorrow of our
past and the joy in our future.

—*Chelle Thompson*

You might have a stress problem if you are stressed because . . .

- traffic has come to a standstill;
- your neighbor's dog is barking;
- you have to give a presentation at work;
- family is coming to stay with you; or
- there is a chance of rain that would ruin your plans.

In dealing with a high-stress lifestyle, if we think most of our stress is caused by external forces, we could be suffering from the "If . . . then" syndrome. "If my job would be different"; "If my spouse was like my neighbor's spouse"; "If my situation was different"; ". . . then I would not be under so much stress." In fact, if you were asked where most of your stress was coming from, I would predict you would say it is from a lack of money or time, your job, or issues at home. You probably would not say, however, that the major cause

7

of your stress is your thinking. Before you throw this book out the window, let me say that your thought life plays a large role in the amount of stress you are experiencing—more than you might imagine.

Believe it or not, we are the cause of most of our stress. Yep, I said it! When it comes to the creation of most of our stress, we are doing it to ourselves. We are our own worst enemy. Epicurus, the Greek philosopher wrote, "It is not the situations in our lives that are causing us stress, but our perception of these situations." Events or situations, either past or present, are not the cause of our sleepless nights, sweaty palms, upset stomach, or stress. We are often under the assumption that it is the external event that is the cause of all our stress. However, it isn't the slow traffic, long lines at the grocery store, work presentations, or family coming to visit that cause most of our stress. It is our interpretation of these events.

Feeling stressed out is a two-fold event. First, we have a stress trigger, such as the long lines or slow traffic. The second factor is perceiving the trigger as being stressful. A formula for stress looks like this:

Stress trigger + negative view of trigger = STRESS

Examples:
Long lines at store + "This is terrible! Only two lines?" = STRESS
Your boss wants to see you + "I'm in trouble!" = STRESS
Your child is pulling on your sweater + "I just want some quiet!" = STRESS

We give power to these external stress triggers by the way we interpret and think about them. If we look at something from one angle, we can experience major stress! If we look at it from another angle, it might cause minimal to no stress!

8

If the causes of our stress were from external circumstances only, then everyone would experience the same response over the same situation, which clearly is not the case. You can introduce ten people to the same scenario, and you will have ten different reactions. What might be stressful to one might not be to another.

Take the term, "Black Friday." To some, this is something to look forward to each year! They love getting out early in the morning and battling the crowds. It's like a big game hunt for them: bagging the elusive bargain, strapping it to the roof of their car, and driving it home with a sense of accomplishment! To me, the thought of getting out before the sun comes up to stand in a long line and fight for something I didn't need in the first place causes me to go weak in the knees with fear! Same scenario, different reactions. It's not the event that causes us stress; it's our interpretation that causes us stress.

So how do we lessen the amount of stress we experience? William James, the father of American psychology wrote, "The greatest weapon against stress is our ability to choose one thought over another."[6] If you want to feel less stress in your life, you need to understand that it starts and ends with your thoughts. You have to think healthier if you want to be healthier.

My dad always said, "Don't make a mountain out of a mole hill." I am sure you have heard that saying too, but so often we DO make a mountain out of a mole hill! We make something huge out of something small by feeding ourselves harmful thoughts that are either misrepresenting or distorting the event in our minds. The more we loop the negative thoughts, the more miserable we become. One of my favorite quotes is by Viktor Frankl, an author and Holocaust survivor. He wrote, "Everything can be taken from

---

[6] http://thinkexist.com/quotation/the_greatest_weapon_against_stress_is_our_ability/330010.html

a man but one thing: The last of human freedoms to choose one's attitude in any given set of circumstances, to choose one's own way."[7]

We need to take responsibility for the thoughts we choose to hang out with. To combat toxic stress and lead healthier lives, to have better relationships, and to deal with life's events in ways that promote success, we need to change from a way of thinking that contaminates our lives to a way of thinking that contributes to our lives. Like Viktor Frankl, regardless of the circumstances, we have to choose our own way.

You can control the amount of stress you experience by choosing how you think. Long before any psychologist came up with how our thoughts affect our lives, King Solomon said, "For as he thinks in his heart, so is he" (Proverbs 23:7 NKJV). King Solomon knew that what we believe is a direct result of our thinking. If our thinking is flawed, then what we believe will be flawed, and what comes out of our mouths will be flawed. It all hinges on our thinking.

However, God is so awesome that He has given us His word to straighten out our thinking! Second Corinthians 10:4-5 reads, "The weapons we fight with are not the weapons of the world. On the contrary, they have divine power to demolish strongholds. We demolish arguments and every pretension that sets itself up against the knowledge of God, and we take captive every thought to make it obedient to Christ."

God tells us that He has given us the weapons we need (in His Word) to not only deal with, but demolish the strongholds in our lives. Not only are we given the tools, we are also to use them. Part of that means to take captive those thoughts that go counter to God's truth!

Billy was a ten-year-old boy who loved to go to his grandmother's

---

[7] https://www.brainyquote.com/quotes/viktor_e_frankl_131417

farm, especially during the summer months. Granny's farm was a great place to play and have adventures. There were acres of land to run on, a pond to swim and fish in, and all sorts of animals to play with. Granny had dogs, cats, a few cows, one pig, and a confused duck. The duck thought it was a dog, and followed Granny around the farm when she did her chores. Granny loved to have that duck sit with her on the porch swing.

One day, Billy was out by the pond skipping stones. He had just let a stone fly when he saw Granny's duck swimming right into the path of the stone. Billy watched in disbelief as the stone hit the duck in the head! Granny's beloved duck went limp in the water.

Billy jumped into the water and swam out to the motionless duck. Bringing it back to the bank of the pond, his fears were realized: the duck was dead. So, out of fear, Billy did what a lot of us would have done—he looked around to see if anyone saw what had just happened, then he started to bury the duck. He grabbed grass, sticks, leaves, and dirt to put over the poor duck. Just when he thought he was finished covering up what he did, he looked up and saw his older sister standing there!

"What are you doing, Billy?" she asked.

"Nothing! I'm not doing anything!" he said.

"You killed Granny's duck, didn't you Billy?"

Billy begged, "Please don't tell Granny! Please don't tell her!"

Billy's sister thought for a moment, then said, "I won't tell her, Billy. It's okay."

With a huge sigh of relief, Billy said, "Thank you! Thank you! I owe you one!"

"I know you do!" she said with a smile.

That night, they were finishing dinner when Granny asked if someone could bring the dishes to the sink. Billy's sister spoke up and said, "Billy will do it, won't you Billy?" Billy was about to argue with her when he saw that grin on her face that reminded him that she had something on him. He thought better of it and agreed to do it.

After he finished the dishes, Granny asked if anyone could feed the animals before it got too dark. Again, Billy's sister spoke up and said, "Billy will help, won't you Billy?"

Who do you think got stuck with every dirty job that night? That's right—Billy! Later that night, Billy was upstairs in his room, getting ready for bed, feeling pretty miserable. Not only was he being haunted by the death of the duck, but now his sister was making him do all the work on the farm. He said to himself that he had had enough and decided to go tell Granny what he did to her duck. He mustered up his courage and went downstairs to talk to her.

He saw Granny sitting on the couch reading a book. She looked up and saw Billy standing there. "Billy, are you okay? Do you need something?" she asked.

Billy broke down crying and said, "Granny. I did something very bad."

She asked what he did. He answered, "Granny, I killed your duck! I didn't mean to! I was skipping rocks when your duck swam in front of the rock! I am so sorry, Granny!"

Granny got up from the couch and went over to Billy to console the broken-hearted ten-year-old with a hug. "It's okay, Billy! I saw what happened."

Billy looked up at Granny. "What? You saw what happened?"

"Yes, honey. I saw you by the pond, and I saw the duck swim in front of the rock. I know it was an accident."

Billy asked, "Why didn't you tell me, Granny?"

She paused, then answered, "I wanted to see how long you were going to allow your sister to hold you in bondage!"

We are like Billy in a lot of ways when it comes to getting ourselves into messes and then allowing the mess to own us. There comes a point when we must choose to deal with our messes instead of allowing them to control us. We can't wait for others to do it for us. We must take action. A rule of thumb is this: God blesses action, not intention. Nowhere in scripture did God ever bless an intention. Blessing followed action.

Every emotion we have, whether good or bad, starts with a thought. What starts in the head comes out in our emotions and then our actions. Take a look at our first recipe, an example of road rage:

Recipe for Road Rage

- I will assume my driving is superior to everyone else's
- I will look for problems
- I will criticize all other drivers
- I will use absolutes such as "should," "must," and "should not"
- I will call the driver names and make threats
- I will play out a scenario in my head in which I berate the driver
- I will "awfulize" and "catastrophize"
- I will aim my frustration at innocent parties

Beat ingredients until mixed thoroughly, then simmer continuously. Serve to others whether they want it or not.

Let's put this recipe into real life. You're driving along on a sunny, Sunday afternoon. You are recalling the wonderful church service you attended and a pleasant lunch with the family. Life is good. Then you look up ahead and see a car wanting to pull out from a side street in front of you. Now comes the internal dialog: "You better not pull out yet! If you want to get hit, go ahead and pull out, goober!" When you're just a few car lengths from it, the car pulls out in front of you, causing you and those behind you to hit the brakes and slow down. The car then turns immediately right onto the next road.

Now your thoughts kick it up a notch or two. "Why?!?! You couldn't wait until we got past you? You just had to pull out! I don't know where you got your license! You've got-to be-kidding!" You then carry on for the next hour, playing a movie in your head of meeting up with the driver in person and giving him a royal chewing out. Physically, your heart beats faster and your blood pressure rises. Your breathing changes and becomes shallower. You feel anxious, and your death grip on the steering wheel is almost bending it. Your pupils dilate, your jaw tightens, and you are ready to jump into a fight, flight, or freeze response. Your adrenalin, noradrenalin, and cortisol hormones have kicked in and created all this stress, but you have nowhere to run and no one to fight.

As you experience the stress hormones raging through your body, not only are you affected physically, but you can aim your frustrations in the wrong direction, snapping at those around you when you get home. The event on the road triggered your physical and emotional reactions, and they can go on for hours, if not for days.

That was just one scenario of what our thought life can do to us, and other situations can create just as much if not more stress. It's okay to experience stress in the short term, but for the long term, this kind of stress becomes harmful.

Unfortunately, we follow this pattern of thought numerous times a day. In the wake of stress, we end up with sleepless nights, upset stomach, and frazzled nerves. No wonder we pop antacids like they're candy. This kind of stress also wakes us up between one and three in the morning with racing thoughts, and we can't go back to sleep until five minutes before the alarm goes off. In the morning, we wake up more tired than when we went to bed, so we hit the snooze button so many times we sound like Ricky Ricardo on the bongo drums.

Work stress, relational stress, financial stress, family stress . . . it seems like we have stress coming out of every orifice of our bodies. If someone asked where all your stress is coming from, you would probably point your finger at one or all the above external sources. I would do the same. All the things mentioned, and much more, contribute to our stressed-out lives, but the one area that causes most of our ills is the one area we fail to take ownership of—our thinking.

Isaac Bashevis Singer writes, "If you keep on saying things are going to be bad, you have a good chance of being a prophet."[8] We have approximately seventy thousand thoughts per day that flip through our little noggins...that's forty-eight to forty-nine self-talk messages per minute. We are what science calls polyphasic thinkers, which means we think about forty thoughts in a heartbeat. The saying that "if you listen to something long enough you start to believe it" is true. Cognitive psychologists, for years, have seen the connection between our thoughts, our emotions, and our behaviors.

Our thinking has a direct effect on our physical, emotional, spiritual, and relational health. In fact, anger, fear, depression, and anxiety are emotions that are preceded by our thoughts. They are preceded by our thoughts. We don't just wake up angry. Instead, we start thinking about something that someone did to us like, "They should not have spoken to me in that tone." The more we ruminate on it, the madder we get. It's not until we get a grip on those internal recipes, that we can get a grip on the stress in our lives that keeps us in bondage.

Thinking makes you what you are, good or bad, right or wrong, real or imagined; it all starts with the attitude of your mind. To quote Williams James again, "The greatest discovery of

---

[8] https://www.brainyquote.com/quotes/isaac_bashevis_singer_155877

my generation is that a human being can alter his life by altering his attitudes of mind."[9]

The sooner we start thinking about our thinking, recognizing that our thoughts have a direct bearing on our spiritual, emotional, physical, and relational health, the sooner and more successfully we can change our unhealthy recipes and their ingredients to ones that promote freedom instead of bondage.

In this book, we will learn to address the thinking errors that are keeping us in bondage. We will learn to replace those thinking errors with thought patterns that not only honor God, but develop a healthier, more fruitful life…a life free from the toxic stress that so adversely affects us. My challenge to you is to not only read this book, but also to put what you read into action!

---

[9] http://www.quotationspage.com/quote/1971.html

CHAPTER THREE

Anxiety

I cry out to God; yes, I shout. Oh, that God would listen to me! When I was in deep trouble, I searched for the Lord. All night long I prayed, with hands lifted toward heaven, but my soul was not comforted. I think of God, and I moan, overwhelmed with longing for his help. You don't let me sleep. I am too distressed even to pray!

I think of the good old days, long since ended, when my nights were filled with joyful songs. I search my soul and ponder the difference now. Has the Lord rejected me forever? Will he never again be kind to me? Is his unfailing love gone forever? Have his promises permanently failed? Has God forgotten to be gracious? Has he slammed the door on his compassion? And I said, "This is my fate; the Most High has turned his hand against me."

Psalm 77:1-10 (NLT)

Experiencing anxiety or panic can be a very frightening experience. You can't eat, you can't sleep, your joints ache, and it's hard to breathe. The man who wrote the psalm above was experiencing a panic attack. In fact, King David dealt with anxiety and depression. You can envision his experience when you read this psalm.

For those going through panic and anxiety, it can feel overwhelming! In this chapter, we will be looking at one of the four horsemen of emotional distress—anxiety. We will uncover the self-talk that plays on a loop in our minds to create feelings of panic. We will also look at replacement messages we can use to combat the feelings of anxiety.

Where Do We Start?

- They might not like me, and that would be awful!
- What if I fail? That would be terrible!
- What if they reject me? I'd be so embarrassed!
- What if I say something stupid? I would look ridiculous!
- They might not want me to be there. That would be awful!
- They might think I am a loser if I don't meet their expectations!
- What if I get bad news? I could not stand it!
- What if I change jobs and it gets worse? I'd be miserable!
- What if they ask me to do something and I can't do it? I'd be such a failure!
- What's going to happen if I lose everything? I could not stand that!
- What if I get hurt? That would be horrible!

These are just a few of the common statements that produce feelings of anxiety and dread. The new Oxford American dictionary describes anxiety as a feeling of worry, nervousness, or unease, typically about an imminent event or something with an uncertain outcome; a nervous disorder characterized by a state of excessive uneasiness and apprehension typically with compulsive behavior or panic attacks.[10]

People who experience anxiety loop statements in their minds such as, "what if" or "they might," and then they add on their anxious thoughts. If what they are worried about actually happened, it would be awful, horrible, terrible, or it will destroy them.

Anxiety is often directed toward the future— "What if I look stupid?" or "I'll never get that promotion anyway, so I don't know why I'm even going to do the interview." At the heart of it all, what we get anxious, stressed, or worried about is fear: fear of what people could do to us or fear of the unknown. Fear is in the driver's seat, and it's taking us down a road that leads to anxiety.

Charles Stanley once wrote, "Fear stifles our thinking and actions. It creates indecisiveness that results in stagnation. I have known talented people who procrastinate indefinitely rather than risk failure. Lost opportunities cause erosion of confidence, and the downward spiral begins."[11] Fear is like the ultimate politician. It speaks out of both sides of its mouth. It tells you not to do something for fear that something negative will happen. Then, when you obey your fear and miss out on opportunities, it condemns you!

Sarryosh Kalwar said, "We are addicted to our thoughts. We cannot change anything if we cannot change our thinking." God tells us not to be afraid 365 times in the Bible! He knew that we needed one for each day of the year! How cool is God! God did not want believers to be slaves to fear. Romans 8:15 says, "The Spirit you received does not make you slaves, so that you live in fear again; rather, the Spirit you received brought about your adoption to sonship. And by him we cry, 'Abba, Father.'" All too often,

---

[10] Oxford Living Dictionaries, https://en.oxforddictionaries.com/definition/anxiety

[11] Charles Stanley Quotes. BrainyQuote.com, Xplore Inc, 2017. https://www.brainyquote.com/quotes/quotes/c/charlessta451693.html, accessed November 1, 2017.

however, we lose sight of God and His promises, and we start to buy into what fear is feeding us. When we let fear take over, we start to experience what I call spiritual hyperventilation.

If you have ever seen someone hyperventilate or have even hyperventilated yourself, you know it can be a very scary experience. Hyperventilation can occur when we become anxious or start to panic. We breathe more rapidly than normal and higher in the chest. When we hyperventilate, it causes a decrease in carbon dioxide in our blood. This decrease can spur a rapid heartbeat. Your heart can feel like it's beating out of your chest. It causes lightheadedness, dizziness, and can also lead to numbness and tingling in extremities such as hands and feet. The mind tricks us into thinking that there is no air and we can't breathe even though we are surrounded by air. To say the least, hyperventilation can cause some disturbing effects on the body that can actually increase our feelings of anxiety and panic.

Spiritual hyperventilation occurs when we tell ourselves, "God is not with us. Where is He?" In reality, God is all around us and His Holy Spirit is in our hearts if we are His followers. We need to slow our breathing and focus on God and His Word, knowing that He is with us, and that He never leaves us or forsakes us! Trust in God to cast out doubt and fear.

Psalm 56:3–4 reads, "When I am afraid, I put my trust in you. In God, whose word I praise—in God I trust and am not afraid. What can mere mortals do to me?" Also, Psalm 56:10–11 says, "In God, whose word I praise, in the Lord, whose word I praise—in God I trust and am not afraid."

People Pleasers

People who are prone to anxiety are almost always people pleasers. People pleasers fear conflict and intense emotions like anger.

They avoid them like the plague! When they start to feel upset or anxious about anything, they tend to sweep the problems under the rug or hide them in a closet in their mind, which is already jam-packed with anxious thoughts. They don't want to upset anyone, (if they do, that would be horrible, terrible, awful!). Their "modus operandi" or immediate response is to push their feelings as fast as they can into that closet, for fear of being rejected or looked down on by others. They do this so quickly and automatically that they are not even aware they're doing it.

I learned a lot from my parents as a child, but there was one thing I wish I would've not learned from my mother. At an early age, the misbelief that "you have to please everyone" was ingrained in me. This misbelief haunted me up until my early thirties. I lived in the mindset that it was a necessity for me to be approved by or loved by everyone. This mindset, not unlike the mindset that "I have to do everything perfectly," is an impossibility; it's never going to happen! When we strive to do the impossible, it starts to erode every area of our life. Sooner or later, we just throw up our hands and give up.

I had to eventually recognize that this was a contaminated mindset. It was impossible for me to please everyone, and it wasn't my job to please everyone. When we make it our responsibility to please everybody, we end up making ourselves a god in their lives, responsible for their happiness! Trying to please everyone and trying to make them happy is like dragging an unconscious man uphill, on ice! You're doing a lot of work, wearing yourself out, and get absolutely nowhere at the cost of your emotional and physical health. I eventually had to choose to not buy into that contaminated untruth I had been telling myself.

I am not saying we shouldn't love and care for others. God tells us to love our neighbor as we love ourselves. We are to minister to and serve one another, but what we must be careful of is caring more about pleasing others than we do about pleasing God. When that happens, we can start to make others our idol.

In my own life, the more I develop my vertical relationship with God, the more it influences my horizontal relationships with others, and I can love them better. I start to treat those around me in a way that pleases God, and I start to speak to others more positively. By aligning my speech and actions with God, I can love others in a way that honors Him.

Two Perspectives on Giants

If ever there was a biblical character who inflicted fear into the hearts of men, Goliath is the supreme example. The book of 1 Samuel tells what happened when Goliath showed up and started mocking the Israelites and demanding they produce someone to fight him. Here we will see two opposing perspectives in dealing with this great crisis. One perspective comes from the Israelites, and the other from David. They both were facing the same obstacle, but they dealt with it altogether differently.

We start with the obstacle in the story, a giant named Goliath: "Goliath stood and shouted a taunt across to the Israelites. 'Why are you all coming out to fight?' he called. 'I am the Philistine champion, but you are only the servants of Saul. Choose one man to come down here and fight me! If he kills me, then we will be your slaves. But if I kill him, you will be our slaves! I defy the armies of Israel today! Send me a man who will fight me!'" (1 Samuel 17:8–10 NLT).

Then the narrative moves to the Israelites' and Saul's perspective of the obstacle: "When Saul and the Israelites heard this, they were terrified and deeply shaken. . .. As soon as the Israelite army saw him, they began to run away in fright (verses 11,24).

When Saul and his army saw and heard the taunts of this

massive monster of a man, they saw him in relationship to who they were. "He is a giant and we are small. He is more than we can handle!"

Then we come to David's view of this obstacle: "David asked the soldiers standing nearby, 'What will a man get for killing this Philistine and ending his defiance of Israel? Who is this pagan Philistine anyway, that he is allowed to defy the armies of the living God?'" (verse 26).

After David got the scoop on what was going on, he went to Saul. "'Don't worry about this Philistine,' David told Saul. 'I'll go fight him!' 'Don't be ridiculous!' Saul replied. 'There's no way you can fight this Philistine and possibly win! You're only a boy, and he's been a man of war since his youth.' But David persisted. 'I have been taking care of my father's sheep and goats,' he said. 'When a lion or a bear comes to steal a lamb from the flock, I go after it with a club and rescue the lamb from its mouth. If the animal turns on me, I catch it by the jaw and club it to death. I have done this to both lions and bears, and I'll do it to this pagan Philistine, too, for he has defied the armies of the living God! The Lord who rescued me from the claws of the lion and the bear will rescue me from this Philistine!'" (verses 32-37).

Unlike King Saul and the Israelite army, David did not see the giant in relationship to who he was. He saw the giant in relationship to who God is. God is big, the giant is small! God was his source.

His reaction was unlike King Saul and his army. Their perspective incited fear, while David's perspective promoted a confidence in God, and he went on to fight and kill the giant. How we perceive something directly affects how that something affects us.

As we battle fear, let us remember these helps we find in David's perspective toward the giant:

1. We have to **recognize the giants we are facing**, which could also include ourselves. Then we have to ask ourselves, "Am I *reacting* to the giant or am I *responding* to it?" Are we cowering in fear, or are we stepping out in God's strength? The Bible never said that David was not afraid. If he was afraid, he stepped out despite his fear.

2. We have to **strip ourselves of all those things that are preventing us from moving forward**. Saul tried to give David his armor. It was not made for him, so it was cumbersome. In order to do what he felt God was asking him to do, David had to take it off and be free of it. If we have unhealthy habits, thought patterns, or relationships in our lives, they are not helping us in our fight.

3. Like David, we have to **continually remind ourselves of all the times God has worked in and through us**. When we do, we start to build the confidence we need to move forward. We need to live in the rich understanding that our source is much greater than our need. God is more than enough to fill any need we have.

4. We need to **move forward in our fight against our giants**. In David's step of obedience, God provided the tools that he needed to defeat Goliath (the five smooth stones), but only when he started moving toward fighting him. When we start to step out, we can be assured that God will provide what we need, when we need it, to deal with the giants we are facing.

Psalm 56:3–4 reads, "When I am afraid, I put my trust in you. In God, whose word I praise—in God I trust and am not afraid. What can mere mortals do to me?" Some fears are normal. These fears help to protect us from actual harm. However, when a fear is based on an illusion and hinders you from doing what God is calling you to do, it acts like a playground bully. Bullies identify their victim's Achilles' heel and continually pommel it until they get their desired response. This is what fear can do to you to keep you from all that God wants for your life.

We all become fearful at one time or another, but we do not have to accept what fear is feeding us as the truth. Fear's goal is to keep us from accomplishing what God desires for us to do.

David wrote, "I sought the LORD, and he answered me; he delivered me from all my fears" (Psalm 34:4). In this verse, David lays out the first step in dealing with our irrational fears. We acknowledge what our fear is and then we immediately turn it over to God, asking Him for His intervention in conquering our fears.

Do you remember the game hot potato? As soon as you get the potato, you pass it off to someone else as quickly as you can. That's the same approach we can take when it comes to dealing with our irrational fears and concerns. All too often, we have a tendency to hold onto our potato, and we end up not letting go of it for hours, days, or a lifetime. And sometimes, if we do give it to God, we grab it back out of His hands.

First Peter 5:7 says, "Cast all your anxiety on him because he cares for you." The word *cast* here is a verb, an action, and it means to "throw something forcefully in a specified direction." It also means to "let loose of, discard, abandon."[12] We are to abandon our cares, our burdens, and our fears into God's hands. If you feel the urge to revisit those cares, burdens, or fears, you can thank God that He has taken them for you instead of allowing yourself to take it back.

---

[12] Oxford Dictionaries, https://en.oxforddictionaries.com/definition/cast

Core Fears

Part of the process of giving our fears to God is to identify what our core fear is. We all have fears, but once we identify what those fears are, they start to lose their grip on us. We can have fears like rejection, abandonment, being seen as defective, being taken advantage of, failure, and the list goes on. These are the internal giants we face. These are the ones we need to place before God. Seeing them in the light of who He is will start to shrink them. He is big; they are small compared to Him. Our fears are never bigger than who God is!

Fears can tend to color how we view ourselves and others in our situation. They can even affect how we perceive what somebody is saying to us. If I have the fear of failure and I am working on something, my wife Kathy can simply ask, "Rick, why are you doing it that way?" If I allow fear to interpret those words, it will translate what she said to, "You are incompetent and are not doing a good enough job to meet the task at hand." And it only goes downhill from there when I react out of my fear filter.

Fear always gives us a distorted lens through which we view the world.

Preparatory Misery

H.P. Lovecraft wrote, "The oldest and strongest emotion of mankind is fear, and the oldest and strongest kind of fear is the fear of the unknown."[13]

Anxiety is predominantly directed toward future events—upcoming interviews, doctors' appointments, presentations, meetings, etc. When we think of these future events, we start to

---

[13] https://www.brainyquote.com/quotes/h_p_lovecraft_676245

loop: "What if I get bad news?" "They might think I'm stupid." "I'll never get that promotion; I'm not good enough!" We prepare ourselves to be miserable; we prepare to fail. We are already experiencing the worst-case scenario, and we are not even there yet. We could be worrying about and dreading a presentation that's a month away. This anxiety robs us of any type of joy or peace in the here and now.

Charles Spurgeon once wrote, "Anxiety does not empty tomorrow of its sorrow's but only empties today of its strength."[14] If I'm not careful, I could worry myself sick today about my dental appointment several months from now! Or I can work myself into a frenzy worrying about a presentation I'm not doing until the end of the year!

My pastor, Tim Harris, once said that "worrying about something is like praying for something you don't want to happen." I call this preparatory misery. We repetitively ruminate about the worst possible outcome for an upcoming event. I once heard that "anxiety is fear in the absence of real danger." There is literally nothing to be afraid of. There is no danger that would cause us to feel healthy fear. The fears are coming from what we imagine will happen. We are locked on negative results, and we're not even there yet.

My family was the poster family for worry, stress, and anxiety. They were consumed with fear, always thinking the worst and assuming the worst about future events. We told ourselves that "it's going to be awful if . . ."; "it would be terrible if . . ."; and "I don't know if I'll be able to stand it if . . ."

However, God instructs us not to worry about tomorrow. In Ephesians 5:15-16 we read, "So be careful how you live. Don't live

---

[14] https://www.brainyquote.com/quotes/charles_spurgeon_132220

like fools, but like those who are wise. Make the most of every opportunity in these evil days" (NLT).

Nowhere in the Scriptures does it say that we are to make the most out of every opportunity that we *long for*. God's Word tells us to make the most out of every opportunity *today*! What are we doing today to make the most out of the opportunities in our spiritual lives, in our relationships, in our vocations, in our ministries?

Instead of seeing the opportunities in front of us, we spend too much time worrying about what's going to be taking place down the road. We fail to live in the here and now, doing what we need to do today, so we miss many opportunities to serve God and love others because we are preoccupied with thinking about tomorrow. When we are with somebody, we're not even with that person because we are too worried about what's going to be taking place in the future.

Practice Living in the Now

We can plan for the future, but we are not to be consumed by it. So, what do we do with the anxiety? How can we not be consumed by the future and our fears?

The first thing we must do when we are starting to feel anxious is to identify the thoughts that are causing it. Ask yourself, "What am I telling myself that is going to be so awful, terrible, horrible?" These thoughts could sound something like, "What if I fail? That would be terrible! What if they reject me? That would be horrible!"

The second step is to challenge the contaminated thoughts about the situation that are causing the anxiety. Challenging these thoughts can sound something like, "Would it really be so terrible if it didn't go the way I planned?" "Would it be so horrible if they didn't interact with me the way I think they should?"

The third step in dealing with contaminated thoughts is to replace them with a healthier line of thinking such as, "It might be unpleasant if they don't talk to me, but it wouldn't be terrible." "It might be annoying if it doesn't go the way I planned, but it will not be horrible. It's not going to destroy me." "Even if what I fear does come to fruition, it will not be terrible. In fact, I know God can make all things work out for the good to those who love Him!"

In order to practice living in the now, we need to change our thoughts. You can use this one-two-three process to develop healthy thoughts and develop a healthier life:

Step 1—Identify
Step 2—Challenge
Step 3—Replace

We must identify those thoughts that are causing us misery (Step 1). Get in their face and challenge them (Step 2). Replace them with thoughts that will contribute to a healthy life instead of contaminating it (Step 3).

Let's put these steps into some real-life thoughts. Here is how the process would work:

Identify *the contaminated thought.* "They are going to think my ideas are stupid, so I'm not even going to try to share them!"

Challenge *the thought.* "I know that is not true!"

Replace *the contaminated thought or lie with a contributing thought.* "I don't know what they will think or do until I share my ideas. They might actually like them, but even if they do not like my idea, it's just their opinion. I will be getting my ideas out there and not living with regret by not sharing them."

Let's look at how Rhonda, a forty-five-year-old client of mine, described how she dealt with emotional distress and anxiety in her life:

My life was full of changes with a move from a place that I considered home for twenty years with my husband and three children. At the same time, my oldest left for college, and I was trying to take care of my mother, who refused to deal with her mental illness. I quickly learned that not properly dealing with life's stressors correctly can lead you to a life of illness and depression.

For years I had been very active. I was a runner, I helped coach, and was involved in every aspect of my children's lives. I had my church family and my friends and a beautiful family and life. Moving made me feel as if I had lost it all. To start all over again was difficult, to say the least.

As I was lifting up and encouraging my children and supporting my husband in his new job, deep inside I was slowly dying and grieving the life I once had. My exercise ceased to exist. I did nothing for myself. I couldn't connect with the schools, and we were trying to find our place in a church once again.

Being the youngest in my family, I was the people pleaser. I was the one who needed to fix everyone and make them better, make them happy, and always keep peace. It is really hard to keep up this pace and "do" all the time.

My mother's bipolar disorder had escalated and was taking its toll on me mentally. I couldn't help her and couldn't fix her either. I didn't understand mental illness. I worried about her, I worried about me, and I worried about everyone and everything. I could not stop the fear and anxiety in my mind. I felt out of control.

At times I couldn't breathe, I couldn't feel my arms. My heart hurt, literally. My body began to shut down. I didn't understand what was going on. I thought I was having a heart attack, but my heart was perfect according to my EKG. I searched to understand what was happening to me physically. There had to be reasons for my dizziness and reasons why I was crippled with fear as I had never been before. I didn't want to leave the house. I didn't want to eat.

An allergic reaction to food caused severe panic attacks after I ate. My husband was afraid to leave me alone. He canceled trips to stay with me.

I prayed that God would just take me home if this is how I had to live the rest of my life. I didn't want to suffer the mental anguish I knew my mom suffered with for so many years. My nights were often difficult. Satan attacked my Achilles heel. He had found my weakness, which was my family. I had such destructive thought patterns about what could happen. All the "what ifs"! Pick, pick, pick, he attacked. So many sleepless nights. My children were my world and Satan knew it. If you could dream it in your head, I had already thought it!

I met a friend at church who literally rescued me. She recognized symptoms in me that were familiar to her and made an appointment for me with Dr. Rick Roepke. He began to share with me how the lies and negative self-talk I had been telling myself were affecting me mentally and especially physically. Understanding the impact of self-doubt and fear and the physical implications that come along with anxiety disorder was quite eye opening.

Once I was able to recognize how the destructive thoughts were keeping me stuck and causing my anxiety and depression to escalate, the healing could begin. I had to stop the pattern of behavior that took me years to develop. I had to stop the negative thoughts or mistruths and replace them with the truth. Then I needed to figure out what may have triggered those thoughts.

I had to learn to take the focus off me and pour it into others, whether by action or prayer. I had to learn to pray harder and cling to Christ like never before. I put myself into this pit and He was there to help pull me out. Through walking, talking, confession, prayer, reading Scripture, and journaling, I began to see a light at the end of the tunnel. Week after week, I discovered new ways to divert my panic and anxiety and lay it down at the foot of the cross. I could not go it alone any longer. My helper was Jesus.

There are still days, if I allowed myself, that I would be consumed by my own negative thoughts. Over and over, I have to put into practice the tools I learned and put on the full armor of God. Through the power of Christ and His sweet Holy Spirit, I make it, one sweet day at a time.

Scriptures for When I Am Worried or Anxious

Use the following verses for the times when worry and anxiety take over. You may even want to try to memorize some of them, so you have an arsenal when you face attacks of worry and anxiety. You can counter-attack with God's Word in your heart.

> Humble yourselves, therefore, under God's mighty hand, that he may lift you up in due time. Cast all your anxiety on him because he cares for you. (1 Peter 5:6–7)

> Do not worry about tomorrow, for tomorrow will worry about itself. Each day has enough trouble of its own. (Matthew 6:34)

> God has not given us a spirit of fear and timidity, but of power, love, and self-discipline. (2 Timothy 1:7 NLT)

> God has said, "Never will I leave you; never will I forsake you." (Hebrews 13:5–6)

> So be strong and courageous! Do not be afraid and do not panic before them. For the LORD your God will personally go ahead of you. He will neither fail you nor abandon you. (Deuteronomy 31:6 NLT)

> So we say with confidence, "The LORD is my helper; I will not be afraid. What can man do to me?" (Psalm 118:6)

> When I am afraid, I put my trust in you. In God, whose word I praise—in God I trust and am not afraid. What can mere mortals do to me? (Psalm 56:3–4)

Paul gives us instructions on what to do with our anxiety in Philippians 4:6-9:

> [6] Do not be anxious about anything, but in everything, by prayer and petition, with thanksgiving, present your requests to God. [7] And the peace of God, which transcends all understanding, will guard your hearts and your minds in Christ Jesus. [8] Finally, brothers and sisters, whatever is true, whatever is noble, whatever is right, whatever is pure, whatever is lovely, whatever is admirable—if anything is excellent or praiseworthy—think about such things. [9] Whatever you have learned or received or heard from me, or seen in me—put it into practice. And the God of peace will be with you.

Paul tells us in verse 6 to give our cares over to God, and to thank Him. In verse 8, we are told to think on things that are true. In the final verse—which is so important—verse 9, Paul says in essence, "Whatever you've heard me say and whatever you have seen me do, put it into practice!" We must continually follow through with these steps if they are to be successful for us.

CHAPTER FOUR

The 3 Ds: Doubt, Discouragement, and Depression

The deepest fear we have, "the fear beneath all fears,"
is the fear of not measuring up, the fear of judgment.
It's this fear that creates the stress and depression of
everyday life.

—Tullian Tehividjian

Aaron was thirty years old when his girlfriend ended their three-year relationship. When he came to see me, Aaron was having a difficult time sleeping and eating. He had lost all interest in the activities he once enjoyed and struggled with staying on task at work, which hurt his productivity. He found himself struggling to get out of bed in the morning. Even trying to take care of his hygiene needs was a chore. Aaron was dealing with depression!

As Aaron and I spoke, he shared with me the situation of the breakup, but also shared his self-talk about the breakup. He felt everything was his fault, that he was a failure, and that he doubted if he would ever find someone who would want to love him. He didn't think he would have much of a future without her in his life.

Aaron was saying to himself, "My life has no meaning. I am nothing now since she left me." His whole foundation for his life had been wrapped up in this young lady. How Aaron viewed himself was directly affected by how she acted or thought. If she was happy, he was happy. If she was upset, he was upset. If she didn't like something, he didn't like it either.

Anytime we allow someone or something to be in the driver's seat of our life, to be the foundation for our life, outside of Jesus Christ our Savior, we are in for a roller coaster ride of pain and disappointment.

We so often buy into the devil's lie that we are only worthwhile if somebody else thinks we are worthwhile or if we perform perfectly. His lies tell me the only worth I have is in performing in a way that pleases everybody else. However, God's love for us is not based on what family we came out of, what we have, or how well we perform. He loves us for *who* we are. There is nothing we can do to make Him love us less, and there's nothing we can do to make Him love us more.

Let's look at the three Ds that can drag us down and keep us from our life with Christ and the purpose He has for us—doubt, discouragement, and depression.

Doubt

We have all heard that misleading voice in our heads: "How can God be so good and deny me what I really want in life? How can God be good and allow my loved one to die? If God is good, why is there so much suffering in the world? If God is so good, why hasn't He taken away these addictions?" These kinds of thoughts create doubt about God's goodness. When we entertain these doubting thoughts, they give way to feelings of discouragement, depression, and even a sense of hopelessness.

Satan is not very creative, but of course he doesn't have to be. We have been believing his deceptions since the fall in the Garden of Eden. When Satan approached Eve, he knew exactly what he was doing. All he had to do was introduce a doubt statement— "Surely

God didn't say you couldn't eat from any of the trees"—when he knew very well that God only forbade them to eat from one tree. Or, "You will not certainly die. God knows that when you eat from it your eyes will be opened, and you will be like God, knowing good and evil" (see Genesis 3:1-5). These purposeful, misleading questions and statements created doubt in Eve, and when she felt the need to correct him, that's when he had her in his trap. Instead of recognizing the deception and dismissing it, she continued in the conversation.

We make the same mistake Eve did. We continue to loop those doubt-inducing thoughts repeatedly in our minds. The more we linger with those thoughts, the more they undermine our confidence in God's goodness, His protection, and our identity in Christ. We can even doubt His love for us, which leads to us doubting God's Word. In Matthew 4, Satan tried to use the same doubt-inducing technique that he used on Eve to get Jesus to doubt His identity.

> The tempter came to him and said, "If you are the Son of God, tell these stones to become bread." Jesus answered, "It is written: 'Man shall not live on bread alone, but on every word that comes from the mouth of God.'" Then the devil took him to the holy city and had him stand on the highest point of the temple. "If you are the Son of God," he said, "throw yourself down. For it is written: 'He will command his angels concerning you, and they will lift you up in their hands, so that you will not strike your foot against a stone.'" Jesus answered him, "It is also written: 'Do not put the Lord your God to the test.'" Again, the devil took him to a very high mountain and showed him all the kingdoms of the

world and their splendor. "All this I will give you," he said, "if you will bow down and worship me." Jesus said to him, "Away from me, Satan! For it is written: 'Worship the Lord your God, and serve him only.'" Then the devil left him, and angels came and attended him. (Matthew 4:3-11)

We could take a lesson from Jesus' protocol when dealing with Satan and his doubt-producing lies. Unlike Eve, who felt she had to argue with Satan, Jesus didn't argue or debate. He simply went to Scripture for the truth, saying, "It is written." For every doubt statement Satan produced, Jesus merely countered it with God's truth.

We have been battling doubt, discouragement, and depression since the beginning of time. You might be dealing with them even now. If you are, my prayer is that this chapter will give you hope.

Over sixty times in the New Testament, God tells us who we are. He says that we are His saints, His beloved children, joint heirs with Jesus Christ, Abraham's seed through Christ Jesus, and we are a new creation through Christ!

Discouragement and Depression

Aaron was using himself as a verbal punching bag, even though we came to find out later in the session that the young lady he had been dating was verbally abusive to him and was involved with another man while she was dating him! Even with that understanding, Aaron was throwing himself under the depression bus by taking responsibility for things he was not responsible for. He needed to be responsible for his own behavior, not the other person's behaviors.

He was so clouded with doubt about himself, his future, whether God really cared for him, and other destructive thought patterns that he failed to see her part in the breakup. He made her the saint and demonized himself. He also failed to see that the relationship was less than ideal in the first place. In fact, the relationship was toxic.

The more he recycled the lies he was telling himself, the deeper he sank into depression. In time, he started to identify the toxic thoughts he was telling himself and how they were robbing him of emotional, physical, and spiritual health. Then he tenaciously chose to replace them with true statements that included God's promises about him and what he was experiencing. That was when depression lost its grip on him.

Elizabeth Wurtzel wrote, "That's the thing about depression: A human being can survive almost anything, as long as they see the end in sight. But depression is so insidious, and it compounds daily, that it's impossible to ever see the end. The fog of depression is like a cage without a key."[15]

Just like doubt often shows up as the precursor to discouragement, discouragement often shows up as the starting point of depression. When we are feeling discouraged, it's because we are more problem-focused than solution-focused. We ruminate on everything that is not going right, what is not happening for us, and what we feel is wrong with the situation. Left unchecked, this leads into feelings of depression and a sense of being defeated.

Depression is not a new illness. People we all know, like Abraham Lincoln, Ernest Hemingway, and even Winston Churchill, suffered from depression. People in the Bible like Elijah, Moses, Solomon, and even King David suffered with depression. Depression is nothing new.

Depression is one of the most common psychological sufferings. As the quote from Elizabeth Wurtzel stated, depression is believing

---

[15] https://www.brainyquote.com/quotes/elizabeth_wurtzel_334889

there is no end in sight; it promotes a sense of hopelessness. Scripture calls it a soul cast down (Psalm 42:5).

Depression usually occurs with provocation: when a loss occurs like death, divorce, or job loss, or difficulties arise around issues like money, health, chronic pain, strained relationships, or failure. Coupled with these losses and difficulties are the thoughts that contribute to or cause depression: "Boy, you aren't very smart. You failed your math exam. What are you doing in college anyway? Look at all the money you're wasting! You'll never make it."

Depression promotes a destructive perspective about ourselves. It devalues the situations we're dealing with: "Life is a drag. Nothing is worth doing. I don't know why I get out of bed anyway!" Depression also disqualifies us from experiencing potential opportunities or positive prospects for the future: "You'll never make it. You'll never be anything. Life is hopeless." The more we repeat these statements, the more we start to believe them, and the more depressed we get.

David Burns, MD wrote, "Every time you feel depressed about something, try to identify a corresponding negative thought you had just prior to and during the depression. Because these thoughts have actually created your bad mood, by learning to restructure them, you can change your mood."[16]

The strange thing about feeling sad or depressed is that we buy into the lies we tell ourselves about things that are not true. This in turn creates misery in our lives. This is where people often get stuck. They continue to repeat destructive self-talk so much that they believe it and even accept it as a way of life. Depression is an illness, yes, but we don't have to accept it as a way of life.

Scripture tells us that we may experience some tough times in our lives, but we do not have to be defined by our difficulties, nor do we have to live in deep depression. Second Corinthians 4:8-9 says,

---

[16] https://www.brainyquote.com/quotes/david_d_burns_618077

"We are pressed on every side by troubles, but we are not crushed. We are perplexed, but not driven to despair. We are hunted down, but never abandoned by God. We get knocked down, but we are not destroyed" (NLT).

Think of what Paul went through without getting depressed, sustained by God's grace. He writes in 2 Corinthians 11:23–28:

> I have worked much harder, been in prison more frequently, been flogged more severely, and been exposed to death again and again. Five times I received from the Jews the forty lashes minus one. Three times I was beaten with rods, once I was pelted with stones, three times I was shipwrecked, I spent a night and a day in the open sea, I have been constantly on the move. I have been in danger from rivers, in danger from bandits, in danger from my fellow Jews, in danger from Gentiles; in danger in the city, in danger in the country, in danger at sea; and in danger from false believers. I have labored and toiled and have often gone without sleep; I have known hunger and thirst and have often gone without food; I have been cold and naked. Besides everything else, I face daily the pressures of my concern for all the churches.

Despite everything Paul went through, he still maintained his trust, his faith, and his focus on God.

Focus

Whatever we're focusing on at any given moment owns us! When my daughter Emily was five years old, she came into our bedroom around 4 o'clock on a Saturday morning and tapped me on the shoulder. When I saw her standing there, fully dressed in her play clothes, I said, "Emily what are you doing, baby girl?" She said, "Daddy, I want to learn to ride my bike." I shook my head groggily and responded, "That's great honey, but can we wait until about eight o'clock? Or better yet, how about after breakfast? Then I'll teach you how to ride!" So, after breakfast, we put her bicycle in the back of the car and went to what I considered a safe place for her to learn how to ride--the empty parking lot of the school.

We got her bike out of the back of the car, put her helmet on, and sat her on the bike. We were about ready to go when she said, "Daddy, you're not going to let go of me, are you? I'm scared that I might fall over if you let go."

"Honey, I am going to keep you safe, and I'll let you know when I let go of the bicycle. Look, there's nothing in the parking lot. It's all good," I said.

She then replied, "What about that light pole Daddy?"

"What about it honey?"

"What if I run into it?"

"Honey," I said, "look all around you. There are no cars. It's an empty parking lot and that's the only light pole out there. You're going to be fine."

So off we went, her peddling as fast as her little legs could peddle, me holding onto the back of her bicycle seat. When I felt confident that she was going to stay up, I said, "I'm letting go, honey. You can do it!" And off she went!

She was doing great, just cruising along! I could hear her laughing as she was riding, and I couldn't help but giggle to myself with pride over her accomplishment! But then I started to notice the direction she was riding. She was heading right for the only thing that was in the middle of acres and acres of nothing: the light pole! I yelled, "Baby, you're doing great, but I want you to turn just a little bit to your left, baby girl. Just a little more honey! HONEY, DADDY SAID TURN!" Then it happened...she hit the only thing in the middle of the wide open parking lot...she hit the light pole!

I ran up to her, as she lay sprawled next to her bicycle and said, "Baby girl, are you all right?" And with a tear in her eye she said, "Yes daddy, BUT I TOLD YOU I WAS GOING TO HIT THAT POLE! I'm going to tell Mommy on you!"

We go in the direction we are focused. Emily had a wide-open parking lot to ride in, but she was so focused on the light pole that it was like a magnet drawing her to it.

David and Michal

The Ark of the Covenant had been away from Israel for twenty-six years. King David was finally bringing the Ark, which housed God's presence, back into Jerusalem. David danced with all his might before the Lord because God's presence was back in Israel!

His wife Michal, however, didn't see God's presence when she looked out the window at the celebration. She didn't experience the joy that Israel was experiencing as the Ark paraded through the city on its way to its rightful place. She was focused on David, dancing in his undergarments, and was repulsed by it. She was focused on how King David was making a spectacle of himself and how he was embarrassing her! She may have even been focused on jealousy as the common girls admired his barely clad, dancing body. In all of this, Michal was focusing on herself. If she were focusing on God and His presence as the Ark was being returned, I think she might have joined King David in his dance, or at least joined in on the celebration.

What we focus on leads us to a certain outcome. King David and Israel were focused on the fact that the Ark was back where it belonged, and their outcome was celebration and joy. Michal was focused on herself and what an embarrassment her husband was to her, which led to the outcome she received—becoming a frustrated and isolated woman who totally missed the presence of God.

How many of us are like Michal? God is doing some amazing things all around us, showing His love, provision, and presence, but all we see is what is not going right. We then end up totally missing out on what He is doing.

What we choose to focus on affects the direction in which we move. In Psalm 42, even King David deals with discouragement and brings the focus of the battle to the forefront. Verses 5 and 6 read, "Why am I discouraged? Why is my heart so sad? I will put my hope in God! I will praise him again—my Savior and my God! Now I am deeply discouraged, but I will remember you—even from distant Mount Herman, the source of the Jordan, from the land of Mount Mizar." There was a battle taking place within David. It would either be his discouragement or his faith in God that was going to win out!

The more we focus on what is not going right in our lives, what's wrong with us, and what we don't have, the more depressed we get. When I continue to tell myself things like, "If I don't have X then it will be terrible. It's always going to be this way, and I can't stand it. If anything bad is going to happen, it's going to happen to me. I don't need to expect anything good in my life. I'm a magnet for anything that can go wrong," then I speak it into existence.

Comparing

We compare ourselves to others by making statements like, "I'll never be good enough. Why can't I be like so-and-so? They seem like they have it all together." When we make comparative statements, we always compare our worst with somebody else's best. We dismiss our good qualities, and we elevate others' abilities, which convinces us that what we do and who we are is insignificant. We start to "should" ourselves with statements like, "I should have," or "I shouldn't have." The more we "should" on ourselves, the more depressed and guilt ridden we become.

The Past

Many of us wish we could go back and change certain things in our lives, but we know we can do nothing to change the past. That's why Paul advises us in Philippians 3:13 to forget what is behind and move forward to run the race set before us.

We did only what was familiar in the past but, now that we know differently, we will do things differently. I can do nothing to change the past, but I can do everything to learn from it, and strive to live a better life. Satan spends a lot of time throwing our past up in our faces, causing us to feel so full of guilt and depression that we are unable to live the way God wants us to live and to achieve those things that are set before us.

Let's look at what Paul said about the past in Philippians 3:12-14: "I don't mean to say that I have already achieved these things or that I have already reached perfection. But I press on to possess that perfection for which Christ Jesus first possessed me. No, dear brothers and sisters, I have not achieved it, but I focus on this one thing: Forgetting the past and looking forward to what lies ahead, I press on to reach the end of the race and receive the heavenly prize for which God, through Christ Jesus, is calling us" (NLT).

Before Paul was Paul, he was Saul. We know what Saul did: he persecuted Christians. In fact, the book of Acts states that he was there when they were stoning Stephen. He was zealous in going after Christians, so that's why Philippians 3 is so important. Paul wrote that he was forgetting what is behind to run the race that was set before him. This tells me Paul was faced with a decision every day—either wake up and reflect on what he did as Saul or focus on what Paul was going to do that day for Christ. Satan uses our past as a distractor to hinder us from moving forward.

When the past starts knocking at the door, I challenge you to choose not to answer it. Instead, refocus yourself on what you have to do today and on who God says you are today. Then affirm yourself with the statement; "I did what I did, and now that I know better, I am doing better. I am stronger by going through what I went through."

When we make ourselves the center of our universe instead of Jesus, we are going to experience disappointment, frustration, anger, and yes, depression.

When We Make Others Our God

When we make others the center of our world, it is like walking on eggshells. When we tell ourselves statements like:

- If he were not in my life, it would be horrible!
- If he leaves me, I am as good as done!
- I can't be happy without her in my life.
- If I am not acting or behaving in a certain way, she won't have anything to do with me, and that would be terrible.
- Her whole mission in life is to make me unhappy.
- He has to treat me the way I want to be treated!

The more we focus on the other person and listen to our internal dialogue, the more miserable we become. In fact, anytime we make something or someone the cornerstone of our life, our joy and happiness will be transient at best. By placing something or someone over God, we are, in fact, committing idolatry. The first commandment says, "You shall have no other gods before Me" (Exodus 20:3 NKJV).

Another way we make someone our god is by telling ourselves that someone makes us feel a certain way. When we make that statement, we are basically saying that we are not in control of our own emotions, but our emotions are in the hands of someone else. By saying that, we elevate that person to a deity role, making them our god. The reverse of that happens when we tell ourselves that we must make everybody happy, or we have to make them feel a certain way. Then, I unknowingly elevate myself to a god-like role because I am putting myself in charge of the emotions of another person. We don't have that kind of power. Now, I can influence someone in either a positive or negative way, but I cannot control that person or how that person feels. That is up to them, just like how I feel is up to me.

Everything in the universe is based on a hierarchy of order. For me, the hierarchy is God, my wife, my children, and then my vocation/ministry. Any time things are not in their right order, we feel off-balance and frustrated. This is also where the "shoulds" come in to play. "They should do XYZ." Or "they shouldn't do XYZ." The more we place "should" statements or thoughts on others, the more resentful and angrier we become.

Instead of throwing "shoulds" all over others, we need to change our thinking to, "I would like it if they would"; "It would be nice if . . . "; or "It's not the way I would have done it, but I am not them."

We Never Stop Affirming Ourselves

We are always affirming ourselves with either negative self-talk or healthy self-talk. We need to actively listen to what we are telling ourselves and try to switch the unhealthy for the healthy, and the mistruth with the truth.

When we are dealing with problems in our life, it is okay to say things like, "I don't like this; this is really not what I expected. I feel sad, and I would like to see it differently." We are not denying the issue we are facing, but neither are we thinking destructive thoughts about the situation and ourselves. We can tell ourselves that something is unpleasant or uncomfortable without making it seem like the end of the world. (We can also be angry about something without condemning, labeling, or belittling ourselves, others, or the situation, by handling our anger in the biblical, healthy fashion.)

Like our friend Aaron, who lost the relationship with his girlfriend, if we lose someone or something important to us, we will experience sadness. However, we do not have to take on the mindset that what or who we lost is the mainstay for life or happiness, or that my life is not worth anything if I do not have that person or that thing back in it. There are times when we don't have control over certain events that happen in our lives, such as the death of a loved one, divorce, or break-up. However, we do have control over the thinking that follows.

Grief and Loss

Often depression surrounds a loss of any kind. When we lose someone or something that was important to us, it can feel like something was stolen from us. In fact, the word bereavement comes from an old English word that means to be robbed of something.[17] When we experience a loss, we will feel the sting. But if we want to recover, it's important for us to get rid of the thought that the only thing worth living for is what or whom we lost. Instead we *grieve* the loss. We acknowledge our emotions. We thank God that He is the source of life and that He, through His grace and mercy, is walking with us through our pain. There is a light at the end of the journey, and He will see us through. Psalm 23 tells us that even

---

[17] https://www.vocabulary.com/dictionary/bereavement

though I walk through the valley of the shadow of death I shall fear no evil. His rod and His staff comfort me.

It is totally possible to experience the full range of emotions in our grief and still desire the healing that can come through the process. Or, we can become stuck in the pain. Second Corinthians 4:16-18 reads, "We do not lose heart. Though outwardly we are wasting away, yet inwardly we are being renewed day by day. For our light and momentary troubles are achieving for us an eternal glory that far outweighs them all. So we fix our eyes not on what is seen, but on what is unseen, since what is seen is temporary, but what is unseen is eternal."

Healing from a loss is a process; it does take time. However, in that loss, we need to honor the love, not the pain or the suffering. Helen Keller wrote about the suffering we experience this way: "Although the world is full of suffering, it is also full of the overcoming of it."[18]

Author William Backus wrote, "A person can lose his/her health, reputation, vision, hearing, legs, hands, even family members, money, homes, physical attractiveness, life goals and plans—and yet recover and go on to live a wonderfully rewarding and meaningful life."[19]

God tells us in His Word that we are more than victorious, that we are more than overcomers (see Romans 8:37). We are in a battle, and in order to be victorious and overcome, we must fight. When we experience loss, our fight is against destructive thoughts and the lies from Satan. In your fight against the destructive thoughts and lies that contribute to depression, remember the three steps that will bring you victory over them:

---

[18] https://www.brainyquote.com/quotes/helen_keller_109208

[19] William Backus, *Telling Yourself the Truth* (Minneapolis, MN: Bethany House Publishers, 2000)

1. **Identify** the harmful thoughts we are telling ourselves about the situation or trigger.
2. **Challenge** those harmful statements.
3. **Replace** the harmful statements with true statements.

Aaron, in dealing with his breakup, was stuck until he started to become aware of, and then challenge, the mistruths he was telling himself:

- "I am nothing without her in my life!" (lie)
- "I know that's not true!" (challenging the lie)
- "It will be hard dealing with the loss of the relationship, but I will get through it. I know my identity is not based on who I'm with; it's based on God and who He says I am!" (replacing the lie with the truth)

A Life of Gratitude

An important tool we can use to get out of doubt, discouragement, and depression is living a life of gratitude! We need to spend more time thanking God for what He is doing in our lives, for how He is providing us, and for who He is. By being grateful, it switches our focus from what's not happening to what is.

Dr. Henry Cloud, author and psychologist, wrote, "We change our behavior when the pain of staying the same becomes greater than the pain of changing."[20] Doubt, discouragement, and depression will try to convince you that you are stuck in the quicksand of the 3 Ds. However, you do have a choice, and there is a way out. It will take a mindset change and effort on your part, but remember, God blesses action, not intention.

---

[20] https://www.goodreads.com/quotes/163723-we-change-our-behavior-when-the-

Scriptures for When I Am Feeling Depressed

God has provided His Word to us for many reasons. One of those reasons is to encourage us. When you are feeling depressed, go to God's Word and prayer. He is the ultimate Comforter and Counselor. Here are a few verses to get you started. You may want to commit some of them to memory so you can remember them when you are not near a Bible and you need a boost of encouragement from the Lord.

All praise to God, the father of our Lord Jesus Christ. God is our merciful Father and the source of all comfort. He comforts us in all our troubles so that we can comfort others. When they are troubled, we will be able to give them the same comfort God has given us. (2 Corinthians 1:3–4 NLT)

And now, dear brothers and sisters, one final thing. Fix your thoughts on what is true, and honorable, and right, and pure, and lovely, and admirable. Think about things that are excellent and worthy of praise. Keep putting into practice all you learned and received from me—everything you heard from me and saw me doing. Then the God of peace will be with you. (Philippians 4:8–9 NLT)

Do not be afraid or discouraged, for the LORD will personally go ahead of you. He will be with you; he will neither fail you nor abandon you. (Deuteronomy 31:8 NLT)

So humble yourselves under the mighty power of God, and at the right time he will lift you up in honor. Give all your worries and cares to God, for he cares about you. (1 Peter 5:6–7 NLT)

The LORD hears his people when they call to him for help. He rescues them from all their troubles. The LORD is close to the brokenhearted; he rescues those whose spirits are crushed. (Psalm 34:17–18 NLT)

I have told you all this so that you may have peace in me. Here on earth you will have many trials and sorrows. But take heart, because I have overcome the world. (John 16:33 NLT)

Don't be afraid, for I am with you. Don't be discouraged, for I am your God. I will strengthen you and help you. I will hold you up with my victorious right hand. (Isaiah 41:10)

CHAPTER FIVE

The Forbidden Fruit

"If we are not actively doing what is right it becomes very easy for the devil to get us to do what is wrong."

—Joyce Meyers

I watched a documentary a while back on how animals are captured and brought to zoos around the world. One of the featured animals was the spider monkey. To catch them, the men made small wooden boxes about the size of a shoe box. The boxes were enclosed on all four sides except for a small circular hole just big enough for a spider monkey's hand to fit. On the other side, they attached a rope. They found the trees where the spider monkeys congregated and attached the boxes to the trees. Inside the boxes, they placed tempting fruit, and then left them there overnight.

The spider monkeys came back to the trees to rest and found the boxes. One of the monkeys smelled the fruit and put his hand into a box through that little hole to retrieve his prize. No worries . . . easy pickings, right? It was like a fruit buffet for monkeys! But the poor little guy soon realized the hole was just large enough to put his hand in, and when he grabbed the fruit in the box, he was unable to pull the piece of fruit and his hand out of the box. All the little guy needed to do was to simply let go of the fruit and he would be able to pull his open hand right out...but he didn't. He refused to let go of the fruit! He pulled at the box and screamed, right up to the time his captors showed up, tranquilized him, and took him away. He was trapped and then imprisoned by the fruit he so desperately refused to let go of.

At first, we think, "Stupid monkey! Just let go of the fruit and you will be okay. You'll be free!" For some reason, the confused monkey would not let go of the one thing that was keeping him trapped and now imprisoned. He bought into the lie that he *must* have the fruit and that he can't let go of it.

But if we were honest with ourselves, we are not so different. We buy into Satan's lie that we "have to have it" and "can't live without it." The "it" is the forbidden fruit. These forbidden fruits are things like adultery, pornography, cheating, lying, gossiping, hatred, revenge, and the list goes on. Did I step on anyone's toes yet? I know I stepped on my own. In this chapter, we will be looking at temptation, habitual sins, and other ways Satan keeps us captive. But we don't have to stay in bondage. God gives us a clear way to free ourselves from Satan's lies and schemes and live life with a free conscience.

In the previous chapter, we took a brief glimpse at Satan in the Garden of Eden. Let's look at this episode in more depth by going back to where the lie started in Genesis 3.

> [1] Now the serpent was more crafty than any of the wild animals the Lord God had made. He said to the woman, "Did God really say, 'You must not eat from any tree in the garden'?"
>
> [2] The woman said to the serpent, "We may eat fruit from the trees in the garden, [3] but God did say, 'You must not eat fruit from the tree that is in the

middle of the garden, and you must not touch it, or you will die.'"

⁴ "You will not certainly die," the serpent said to the woman. ⁵ "For God knows that when you eat from it your eyes will be opened, and you will be like God, knowing good and evil."

⁶ When the woman saw that the fruit of the tree was good for food and pleasing to the eye, and also desirable for gaining wisdom, she took some and ate it. She also gave some to her husband, who was with her, and he ate it. ⁷ Then the eyes of both of them were opened, and they realized they were naked; so they sewed fig leaves together and made coverings for themselves.

Not only does Satan use lies that foster negative emotions such as depression, anxiety, self-condemnation, and fear to keep us in bondage, he also uses forbidden fruit to keep us trapped!

The fruit that Satan used to tempt Adam and Eve can represent any temptation we could be struggling with that stems from fleshly desires, such as lust, envy, greed, revenge, and pride. Often the lie will start with, "If you will just . . . then you will get . . ."

"If you will just look at these images online, then you will feel amazing."

"If you will just tell one person that story you heard about your co-worker, it will make you look better than her and they will think about you for that promotion."

Temptation, just like any other of Satan's lies, distorts our sense of self, dehumanizes others, minimizes our responsibility, and produces destructive outcomes. This is not unlike what took place in the garden. How easily we get sucked in!

But it takes more than just a temptation. Tempting us is Satan's role. It takes giving in to the temptation—that is the part we play. Franklin P. Jones writes, "What makes resisting temptation difficult for many people is they don't want to discourage it completely."[21] Let's look at the process that leads to sin.

The Hook

In the Garden of Eden, Satan threw out the hook in the first stage of the process. He asked Eve, "Did God really say you must not eat fruit from any of the trees in the garden?" This hook promotes doubt about God and His goodness—basically implying that if God was truly good, He would let you have whatever you want! The hook is also designed to get the victim thinking about the fruit. After the serpent planted the thought, Eve started the dialogue with him by trying to correct him. The best thing Eve could have done at that point was to just walk away and not engage him. The longer the conversation went on, the more he had her hooked!

Fantasizing

After dialoguing with Satan, Eve saw that the tree was beautiful, its fruit looked delicious, and she wanted the wisdom it would give her.

At this second stage, we start fantasizing about what it would be like to carry out the temptation. We begin rationalizing or justifying why we should have or do what we are fantasizing about: "Who will know?" "What will it hurt? It just involves me." "They

---

[21] https://www.brainyquote.com/quotes/franklin_p_jones_161914

deserve what they're going to get!" "My spouse doesn't understand me like they do!"

Acting Out the Fantasy

"So she took some of the fruit and ate it. Then she gave some to her husband, who was with her, and he ate it, too" (verse 6).

The third stage is the worst; we give in to the temptation and commit the sin. Sin never affects just the one committing it. It can have long term consequences, leaving a wake of destruction in its path. Adam and Eve's act of disobedience ushered sin into the world. It has left a path of destruction so wide and evil that we are still feeling the effects today. It will continue until God wipes it from the face of the earth. What a day that will be! No more sin, no more evil, no more temptation. But until that day comes, we need to know how to deal with it and how to stand up to Satan's attacks.

Walk, Stand, Sit

In Psalm 1:1 we read, "Blessed is the man who walks not in the counsel of the ungodly, nor stands in the path of the sinners, nor sits in the seat of the scornful." This verse illustrates the progression into temptation and how our enemy traps us. First, we walk with Satan, then stand in his presence, then we just sit right down and wallow in it.

Walk = Hook (We are in control at this point—we can walk the other way, or we can walk with Satan.)

Stand = Fantasizing (We start to lose control as we think about the forbidden fruit.)

Sit = Acting Out the Fantasy (The temptation is now in control and we have completely given in.)

I heard it once said that temptation usually comes in a door that was deliberately left open. One way to close that door is to shift our focus. Let's look at how we can make that choice.

Shift Your Focus

We need to shift our thinking so we can open our eyes and see the temptation for what it really is—a trap. Temptation always shows up right before God is about ready to do something in and through you. Satan wants to derail you from experiencing the blessings of God. Satan wants to catch you in his snare so that you are no good to God.

The best stage to shut Satan down and combat the temptation is at the walking stage. We can shut down the conversation we're having with the temptation and stop playing the movies in our heads by switching our thinking to God's truths. Psalms 1:2-3 says, "But his delight is in the law of the LORD, and in His law he meditates day and night. He shall be like a tree planted by the rivers of water, that brings forth its fruit in its season, whose leaf also shall not wither; and whatever he does shall prosper." If we entrench ourselves in God's Word, we will be strong and fruitful. We can use this against Satan's attacks. If we are not in God's Word, we wither and weaken. This is no condition to be in if we want to fight off temptation. We need to have God's Word firmly planted in our minds so we can use it as the Sword God has provided for us. Later in this chapter, I will give you words from the Bible you can throw back at Satan as you are walking away from his temptations.

Another way to shut down the conversation with temptation is to seek out an accountability partner, someone you trust enough to be real with, and who will be honest with you about what you're dealing with. (If what you are struggling with is more than what an accountability partner can help you with, seek out a pastor or professional who could walk with you through your journey of breaking free from sin.)

In the story of Jesus and Lazarus (see John 11:1-44), Lazarus had been dead for four days and put into a tomb. Jesus came on the scene and told them to roll away the stone. He then called out, "Lazarus come forth," and at that point Lazarus was born again! How did he come out of the tomb? He was still wrapped in grave clothes. You and I could be born again and yet still be walking around in grave clothes too! These grave clothes can represent such things as fear, insecurities, addictions, and self-loathing.

Jesus then looked to those next to Lazarus and said, "Loose him and set him free!" Jesus wants us to be set free, and He knows there are occasions when we can't do it by ourselves. Like Lazarus with his grave clothes, we need the assistance of others to help us get through the things we are struggling with.

HALT

Sometimes temptations show up when we feel on top of the world. Sometimes they show up when we are at a low point, when we are stressed, or struggling in a certain area. Using the acronym HALT, we can identify what those areas are:

H=Hungry When we are hungry, we can have a decrease in blood sugar, which can lower our defenses to temptation.

A=Angry When we feel we have been wronged or threatened, it can elicit a fight, flight, or freeze response.

L=Lonely When we feel disconnected, abandoned, overlooked, or insecure, we can become vulnerable to lies and schemes.

T=Tired When we are tired, we tend to become more irritable, irrational, and impulsive. Vince Lombardi said, "Fatigue makes cowards of us all."[22]

Before giving in to temptation, we need to ask ourselves if we are hungry, angry, lonely, or tired. This allows us to pause before acting.

---

[22] http://www.great-quotes.com/quote/46503

"I am . . ."

Use "I am" statements to remind yourself that giving into temptation is not who you truly are. The words "I am" are the two most powerful words we could use to start any statement. "I am a failure. I am not good enough. I am less than. I am always going to be stuck. I am unlovable." The more we recycle those unhealthy "I am" statements, the more disconnected, hopeless, depressed, and anxious we become, and then we are more likely to give in to the temptation we are struggling with.

That is why it's so important for us to change out those unhealthy "I am" statements to those "I am" statements that align with God's Word. When you are affronted with negative "I am" statements or tempted by Satan to disobey God in sin, here are some true statements you can use to combat him.

My Identity in Christ!

I am redeemed and forgiven – Ephesians 1:6-8
I am free from condemnation – Romans 8:1
I am a new creation – 2 Corinthians 5:17
I am God's workmanship – Ephesians 2:10
I have been given the mind of Christ – 1 Corinthians 2:16
I've been justified, made righteous – Romans 5:1
I have received fullness in Christ – Colossians 2:10
I am a child of God—He is my Father – 1 John 3:1-2
I have been adopted by God – Romans 8:15
I am hidden with Christ in God – Colossians 3:3
I am chosen of God—holy, loved – Colossians 3:12
I am a child of light, not darkness – 1 Thessalonians 5:5
I am a partaker of Christ – Hebrews 3:14
I am a member of the royal priesthood – 1 Peter 2:9

I am light in the world – Matthew 5:14

I have been given spiritual authority – Luke 10:19

I am a minister of reconciliation – 2 Corinthians 5:18-19

I am a temple of God – 1 Corinthians 3:16, 6:19

I am reconciled to God – 2 Corinthians 5:18

I am a saint – Ephesians 1:1; 1 Corinthians 1:2; Philippians 1:1

I am a fellow citizen in God's kingdom – Ephesians 2:19

I am rescued from Satan's dominion – Colossians 1:13

I would encourage you, for the next thirty days, to read each one of these "I am" statements out loud as a declaration of who you truly are.

Scriptures to Combat Temptation

In 1 Corinthians 10:13, we read, "No temptation has overtaken you except what is common to mankind. And God is faithful; he will not let you be tempted beyond what you can bear. But when you are tempted, he will also provide a way out so that you can endure it." Below are some short Scriptures to memorize. When you tuck these verses in your heart, you are tucking the mighty Sword of God's Word into your belt. When Satan comes at you with temptations, you can come back at him with God's own words. Remember, "Your word I have hidden in my heart, that I might not sin against You" (Psalm 119:11). Use this powerful weapon as it was intended. It will help you in your battle against sin.

- Hate what is evil; cling to what is good. Romans 12:9
- Keep your tongue from evil and your lips from telling lies. Psalm 34:13
- Turn from evil and do good; seek peace and pursue it. Psalm 34:14

- Do not set foot on the path of the wicked or walk in the way of evildoers. Proverbs 4:14
- Do not turn to the right or the left; keep your foot from evil. Proverbs 4:27
- To fear the Lord is to hate evil; I hate pride and arrogance, evil behavior and perverse speech. Proverbs 8:13
- Truly the righteous attain life, but whoever pursues evil finds death. Proverbs 11:19
- The wise fear the Lord and shun evil. Proverbs 14:16
- Flee from sexual immorality. All other sins a person commits are outside the body, but whoever sins sexually, sins against their own body. 1 Corinthians 6:18
- But you, man of God, flee from all this, and pursue righteousness, godliness, faith, love, endurance and gentleness. 1 Timothy 6:11
- Flee the evil desires of youth and pursue righteousness, faith, love and peace, along with those who call on the Lord out of a pure heart. 2 Timothy 2:22
- Submit yourselves, then, to God. Resist the devil, and he will flee from you. James 4:7
- The Lord rewards everyone for their righteousness and faithfulness. 1 Samuel 26:23
- I will give thanks to the Lord because of his righteousness; I will sing the praises of the name of the Lord Most High. Psalm 7:17
- The Lord loves righteousness and justice; the earth is full of his unfailing love. Psalm 33:5
- In your righteousness, rescue me and deliver me; turn your ear to me and save me. Psalm 71:2
- Your righteousness, God, reaches to the heavens, you who have done great things. Who is like you, God? Psalm 71:19

- Lord, hear my prayer, listen to my cry for mercy; in your faithfulness and righteousness come to my relief. Psalm 143:1
- I walk in the way of righteousness, along the paths of justice. Proverbs 8:20
- In the way of righteousness there is life; along that path is immortality. Proverbs 12:18
- The Lord detests the way of the wicked, but he loves those who pursue righteousness. Proverbs 15:9
- Whoever pursues righteousness and love finds life, prosperity and honor. Proverbs 21:21
- Blessed are those who hunger and thirst for righteousness, for they will be filled. Matthew 5:6
- You have been set free from sin and have become slaves to righteousness. Romans 6:28
- Stand firm then, with the belt of truth buckled around your waist, with the breastplate of righteousness in place. Ephesians 6:14

Take a few minutes to read through this list of verses. Pray and ask God to help you choose five verses to memorize. Write your five verses below to start the process of memorization. To get them into your heart and mind, use any memorization technique you are comfortable with. You may wish to write or print them out and place them somewhere you will see them daily—on your bathroom mirror, on your phone, on your refrigerator, or wherever would help you most. When you come across temptation, you can quote your five verses, turn yourself in the opposite direction, and have the victory.

My five verses for countering Satan's attacks:

1. _____

_____

2. _____

3. _____

4. _____

5. _____

It's Your Choice

Life is a series of choices. At any given moment, on any given day, we are at a crossroad of choices. What we choose to occupy our thoughts and the choices we make take us down certain paths, and these paths always have outcomes. They will either take us down a path that leads to healthy living or a path that leads to heartache. The thoughts you have and the actions you take are either going to align you with God, or they're going to move you in the opposite direction and align with Satan. It's your choice! It's up to you which path you choose, so choose wisely.

If we know we are headed down the wrong path, we must work tenaciously to get off that path and create a new one. It's hard work.

It is grueling at times. There may be days when you counter sinful thoughts with God's Word over and over all day long. But when you have a clear conscience and you are walking with God on His path, the peace and joy you experience is worth all the hard work!

"Watch and pray so that you will not give in to temptation. For the spirit is willing, but the body is weak" (Matthew 26:41 NLT).

Now that we have a strategy for dealing with sin and temptation, let's look at the process that can help us even more with temptation, stress, anxiety, and the three Ds—doubt, discouragement, and depression.

CHAPTER SIX
The Thought Results Process

"You fool, Victor Frankenstein of Geneva! How could you know what you had unleashed? How was it pieced together? Bits of thieves? Bits of murderers? Evil stitched to evil stitched to evil. God help your loved ones."
—*Mary Shelley's Frankenstein (1994)*

Since the early 1930s, society has had a love affair with monsters—The Blob, Dracula, The Thing, The Creature from the Black Lagoon, Godzilla, the Walking Dead, and yes, our buddy Frankenstein. We flock to horror movies by the millions to have an opportunity to be scared out of our seats! Afterward, we spend days sharing with others the most terrifying moments of the show, especially when we jumped out of our seats, covered our eyes, or turned our heads away. One of the nice things about watching a scary movie or scary TV show is that when we get scared, we can leave the theater, change the channel, or leave the room if it gets too bad.

The real truth, however, is that we don't need to go to a monster movie or watch ghost shows, because we are being haunted by thoughts that seem to be lurking in every corner of our minds, and we feel like we can't get away from them! Like Victor Frankenstein of Geneva, how could we have known what we had unleashed?

How was it pieced together? Bits of self-condemnation? Bits of comparing yourself to others? Bits of assuming? Bits of temptations? Evil stitched to evil stitched to evil. God help you and your loved ones!

Robert Conklin put it like this:

I Am Your Master

I can make you rise or fall.

I can work for you or against you.

I can make you a success or failure;

I control the way you feel and the way you act;

I can make you laugh . . . work . . . love.

I can make your heart sing with joy . . . excitement . . . elation.

Or I can make you wretched . . . dejected . . . morbid.

I can make you sick . . . listless . . .

I can be a shackle . . . heavy . . . attached . . . burdensome.

Or I can be as the prism's hue . . . dancing . . . bright . . .

fleeting . . . lost forever unless captured by pen or purpose;

I can be nurtured and grown to be great and beautiful . . .

seen by the eyes of others through action in you;

I can never be removed . . . only replaced.

I am a THOUGHT.

Why not know me better?

All of us experience negative thoughts at one time or another. We all have thoughts that creep in and try to trip us up. However, for some of us, this can be a daily experience, looping negative thoughts so much that they own us. So, the question is, where did we pick up these negative, irrational thinking styles?

Thinking styles come from three areas: our parents' thinking, our learning experiences, and our cultural beliefs and expectations. Let's explore these ideas a little more.

1. **Our Parents' Thinking**—Often we pick up negative thinking patterns from our parents. A young woman in my office once stated that she was "eaten up with worry." I asked several questions. One was "Why?" She looked at me and repeated "Why?" She thought more about the question, then said, "I guess because my mom worried, and now that I think about it, my granny was always in a state of panic. So, I guess the answer to your question is that I come from a long line of worriers!"

   Our parents often don't realize they are planting seeds of irrational thinking in us. They are unaware that their thoughts are unhealthy, so they don't pass on other options about how to think about things. Even if they don't directly tell us how to think, we pick it up by watching their behavior and how they handle issues and situations they are facing.

   When I was growing up, I saw my parents argue and fight when the phone rang. Every time the phone rang, they would not let us answer it out of fear that it was a bill collector. So, as the phone rang, they yelled at each other about not having enough money or overspending. When I finally left home around the age of seventeen, whenever my phone rang, I became like Pavlov's dog and experienced negative thoughts and a sick feeling in my stomach. My folks passed on their irrational thinking to me, and the irony is that, at that time, I didn't have any bills!

2. **Our Learning Experience**—During our lives we have many experiences, and the outcome of those experiences can be good or not-so-good. These outcomes contribute to our thinking patterns. For example, if we have experienced a trauma in our life, it can affect our interpretation of a situation. If we, or someone we love, were badly hurt in a car accident, we can experience negative thoughts about traveling by car. We can jump to the worst-case scenario, thinking, "What if I don't make it?" Due to the trauma experienced earlier in life, possibility turns into probability.

3. **Cultural Beliefs and Expectations**—The culture in which we were raised plays a major role in our development of healthy or unhealthy thinking patterns. Some of those thinking patterns can lead us down a problematic behavioral path. Performance can be one of those cultural expectations that we pick up, leading us to feel overwhelmed and stressed out, which can lead to becoming paralyzed and not even trying. Many young girls, and even boys, fall into the trap of thinking that they must have perfect bodies, skin, and hair, and wear all the right clothes. Magazines, movies, and TV are the main contributors to this, where models and actors are photo-shopped and airbrushed to appear perfect. This often influences young people to be overly body-conscious, which can lead to eating disorders.

The Results Process

Often, we look first to our behavior when we want to change something about ourselves or about our lives. In fact, we have heard others (teachers, parents, spouses, etc.) say to us, "You'd better change your behavior, or else!" We work on our behavior, and we might successfully change for a week or two. But then, we fall back into old patterns. We, and those wanting us to behave differently, end up frustrated and at odds with each other. Just focusing on our behaviors is not enough for true, long-lasting change. Our real focus should be on the thoughts that create our behaviors.

We again have an estimated seventy thousand thoughts per day, and around 48-49 self-talk statements per minute. We are polyphasic thinkers. That means we can think multiple thoughts at any given moment. Whatever you are thinking about in any given moment owns you. Whether good or bad, right or wrong, real or imagined, you are influenced by that thought. James Aller wrote, "You are today where your thoughts have brought you; you will be tomorrow where your thoughts take you."[23]

That is why it is so important to be aware and purposeful in our thinking. In order to do this, we need to understand the thought results process. It looks like this:

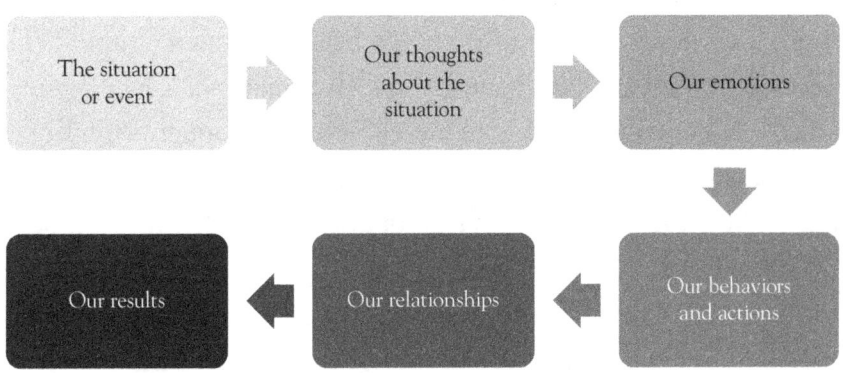

We go through this results process hundreds, if not thousands of times each day. Every emotion we experience, every action we take always follows this cycle. We do not operate independently from it. The more we understand how it operates and influences

---

[23] https://www.brainyquote.com/quotes/james_allen_133802

us, the more aware and purposeful we can be in influencing the process for our benefit.

The first part of the results process is the *situation or event*. This is any situation in life we are dealing with or any event that has happened or will be happening. Situations could be slow traffic, an unexpected bill or expense, noisy neighbors, barking dogs, yelling spouses, misbehaving kids, or increased responsibility at work. Future events might be something like an upcoming presentation at work, an upcoming test, a dental appointment, the in-laws coming for a visit, Christmas, or other holidays. Past events could be past relationships, being called a name, being bullied, past trauma, job loss, or moving.

The second part of the results process is our *thoughts about the situation or event*. Any emotion or behavior starts with a thought. When we have thoughts about what we are facing, they are either positive or negative. Negative thoughts sound like, "I can't stand this"; "I can't"; "I should have known better"; "I am so stupid"; "I'll never get it right"; "Not again!"; "It's all hopeless"; "Once again I failed"; "This is awful"; "I hate myself." Positive thoughts might be, "What's done is done, move on"; "It will be okay"; "God calls me His child"; "I look forward to that opportunity"; "It will work out"; "What steps do I need to take?"

The third part of the results process is our *emotions*. Our emotions are by-products of our thoughts. Negative emotions such as anger, depression, resentment, anxiety, fear, panic, hate, stress, and feeling overwhelmed are a direct response to the negative thoughts we are looping in our minds. The longer we loop them, the more intensely we feel the emotions. The same is true for positive emotions, such as peace, joy, happiness, love, excitement, and contentment when we focus on healthy thoughts. And like the negative ones, the more we loop the positive thoughts, the more we experience the positive emotions.

The fourth part of the results process is our *behaviors*. Our behaviors are a direct result of the emotions we are experiencing. Either negative or positive, the behaviors are the by-product of the emotion.

Fifth is our *relationships*. They are influenced heavily by our behaviors. The ways we act cannot help but influence how people interact with us. If our emotions are bubbling beneath the surface, they are bound to come tumbling out at the first people who cross our paths. And they will possibly affect every person who crosses our paths the rest of the day.

This leads to the last part of the process—*our results*. The results we experience, whether positive or negative, come directly from the previous parts of the process. If your behaviors are bad (blowing up at our co-worker), your relationships suffer (everyone who saw the argument with formulate a low opinion of you), and your results will follow (your boss decides to give that promotion to someone who can manage their anger instead of you).

Here's an example of the complete results process:

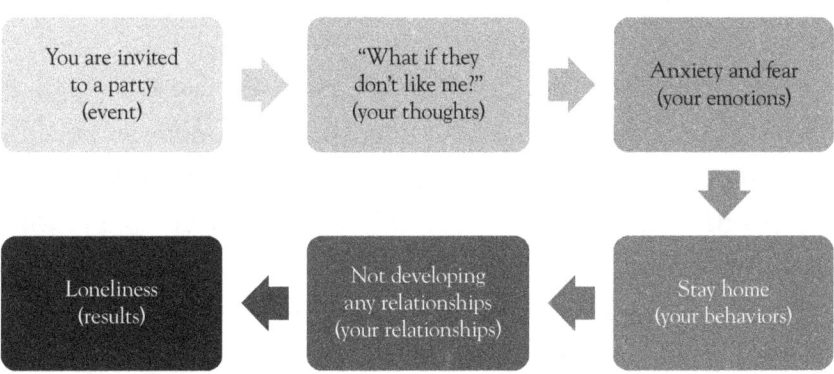

It is so important for us to not only understand this process, but to actively influence it so our results are ones that we want. To change the result, our point of focus in this results process needs to be our thoughts. Our thoughts are the key ingredients in our life's recipes. If we change them, we change the rest of the cycle and our recipes change. If we don't, it should never surprise us when we are constantly getting the same result! We can't change goulash to brownies without changing the ingredients.

In dealing with the monsters we create in our minds, we need to rethink our thinking. Not only do we need to understand where our thoughts come from, but we need to know that the results we get are directly affected by our thought cycles.

As a man thinks in his heart, so he is; and as he continues to think, so he will remain (see Proverbs 23:7).

Contaminating Versus Contributing

Along with our understanding of the results process, we also need to understand that our thoughts fall into one of two categories. Contaminating thoughts are parasitical in nature, sucking the life right out of us. Contributing thoughts produce health, hope, and energize us. Simply put, our thoughts are either contaminating our lives, our relationships, and our situations, or they are contributing to our lives, our relationships, and our situations.

Contaminating thoughts are like parasites, like ticks feeding off you. The thoughts that fall under the contamination heading are pessimistic, focusing on the downside of everything. They label and belittle us and others. They only see what is wrong and what is not happening instead of the good and the possibilities. They only focus on the negative. Looping contaminating thoughts about ourselves, others, and our situations has a proven track record. It causes us to become more depressed, anxious, angry, and fosters feelings of doubt, discouragement, and dread. Contaminating thoughts only expect the negative, see only the negative, and cause us to judge ourselves and others harshly. Contaminated thinking leaves us physically, emotionally, and spiritually depleted.

Contributing thoughts, on the other hand, promote a healthier life and a more enriching and positive view of ourselves. They promote stronger relationships. They act as a catalyst for productive outcomes. Contributing thoughts are not fluffy, Pollyanna thoughts or head-in-the-sand thinking. They are merely more optimistic and realistic in nature. For example, I might face some obstacles in my life, but I know that with God's help, I can figure it out. This approach is more believable. It is, by far, a healthier approach to ourselves, our relationships, and the situations we are facing.

Take a look at these contaminating versus contributing thoughts:

Thoughts About Myself

CONTAMINATING	CONTRIBUTING
It doesn't make any difference what I do, I won't get that promotion.	I am going to work each day as unto the Lord. Hard work pays off. Even if I don't get the promotion, I can be satisfied that I did a good job.
What is the matter with me? I am so stupid!	I am learning, and I know how to handle difficulties.
Once again, I have fallen short! I will never be good enough!	I am going to step back up to the plate and try again. This does not define who I am.

Thoughts About Others

CONTAMINATING	CONTRIBUTING
They are out of their minds!	They see things differently.
They just don't get it!	They disagree.

CONTAMINATING	CONTRIBUTING
It's all their fault!	What was my role?

Thoughts About Situations

CONTAMINATING	CONTRIBUTING
Who's to blame?	What's done is done! How could I approach this differently?
Oh no! Not this again! This is horrible!	It could be better, but I have seen this before, and we will get through it!
It will never be perfect!	There is no perfection, but I will give it my all!

All of us need to be more intentional about our thought lives. Remember, whatever you are focusing on in any given moment owns you! Imagine walking into a room and seeing a sofa against the wall. Seated on opposite ends of the sofa are two figures—one is named *Contribute* and the other is named *Contaminate*. As soon as you walk into the room, they both start speaking to you, competing for your attention. They speak at the same volume and speed. At first, it sounds like chaos. However, as you choose one voice to focus on, you hear more clearly, and the other voice fades to the background. You are now in tune with the voice you are focused on. The more you listen to one or the other, the more you are either contaminating or contributing to your life by what you think!

Making the Choice

We all have the ability to choose what perspective to hang out with. The nice thing about hanging out with the contributing thoughts is that not only does it assist in better outcomes, but it also gives us healthier coping strategies. To quote Victor Frankl, "Between stimulus and response there is a space. In that space is the power to choose our response. In our response lies our growth and our freedom."[24]

It's a Progression

Psalm 1:1 reads, "Blessed is the man who walks not in the counsel of the ungodly, nor stands in the path of sinners, nor sits in the seat of the scornful" (NKJV). When you read this verse, you see a progression: walk, stand, sit—going deeper and lower as the verse continues. In the last chapter, we saw how this progression leads to sin. This verse also illustrates the progression of our thoughts.

Walk—a negative/contaminating thought shows up out of nowhere, invading your mind. Instead of dismissing the contaminated thought, we start to entertain it by rolling the thought around in our minds. *Stand*—the longer we stand, or entertain the thought, the more that negative thought starts to own us. Then we come to the *Sit* stage. We are not only locked onto that thought, we are also experiencing physical distress. We get that feeling in the pit of our gut, we start clenching our teeth, our breathing changes and becomes shallower, and then our actions start to reflect our contaminated thoughts. The more we sit, the more toxic it becomes.

Walk-stand-sit might look like this in the thought process:

---

[24] https://www.brainyquote.com/quotes/viktor_e_frankl_160380

You are asked to lead a six-week class at church. At first, you are excited about the opportunity. Then, the initial thought begins, "You're not smart or good enough to lead it" (walk). Instead of dismissing it or changing the thought, you spend time with it. "I have never done anything like that before! Why should they, or anyone, listen to me?" (stand). Then it moves into the last stage of the progression. "I can't do this! I will never be smart enough! I am not as good as the others! I CAN'T STAND THIS! WHY DID HE ASK ME? HE KNOWS BETTER! I feel sick! I'm going to tell him I can't!" (sit). It is important to understand that the sooner we intervene by dismissing the negative thought and replacing it with a contributing thought, the better off we will be. If I were to write the formula for our thoughts, it would look like this:

What we focus on + time spent focusing on it = the outcome

But God gives an alternative to Psalm 1:1 in the next verses! "But his delight is in the law of the LORD, and in His law he meditates day and night. He shall be like a tree planted by the rivers of water, that brings forth its fruit in its season, whose leaf also shall not wither; and whatever he does shall prosper" (Psalm 1:2-3 NKJV).

What we focus on (the law of the Lord) + time spent focusing on it (meditates on it day and night) = the outcome (bears fruit, healthy leaves, prosperity)

Instead of entertaining and hanging out with these contaminating thoughts, we need to immediately choose to dismiss them and replace them with contributing thoughts. God's Word is full of alternative points of focus that lead us down a path of healthy thinking. The chapters to come will show more in-depth ways to recognize the contaminating thoughts toward ourselves, others, and our situations and give us ways to dismiss and replace them with thoughts that contribute to ourselves, others, and our relationships and situations.

PART TWO
Changing Your Life's Recipes

You were taught, with regard to your former way of life, to put off your old self, which is being corrupted by its deceitful desires; to be made new in the attitude of your minds; and to put on the new self, created to be like God in true righteousness and holiness.

—Ephesians 4:22-24

CHAPTER SEVEN
Stop Having Coffee with Satan

*Then I heard a loud voice shouting across the heavens,
"It has come at last—salvation and power and the
Kingdom of our God and the authority of his Christ.
For the accuser of our brothers and sisters has been
thrown down to earth—the one who accuses them
before our God day and night."*

Revelation 12:10 NLT

Imagine you are going into a coffee house to have coffee with someone you have been meeting with for years. You enter the coffee house, look around, and spot him. As always, he is as reliable as clockwork, willing to meet you whenever you call on him. He already has his coffee and is waiting at the table. You get your coffee and go sit down. He smiles, and before you can take your first sip, he proceeds to bring up every wrong you have ever done, every mistake you've ever made. He adds to your list of sins what a miserable individual you are and that you are the biggest loser that ever walked the face of the earth (and I'm not talking about the TV show). He reminds you why you are so inept at everything you do, how you are such a failure, and if people really knew you, they wouldn't have anything to do with you—you are a fake! He also adds, with delight, that there is absolutely no way God could ever use you for anything. Because of your past, you're not good enough to be part of what God is doing.

An interesting yet disturbing observation about your coffee mate is this: the more you allow him to speak, the more gleeful he becomes, and he increases in size. At the end of your time with him, you get up to leave and he says, "Same time tomorrow?" You nod yes, and off you go, feeling worse about yourself than you did when you walked into the coffee house.

It's amazing how many of us will continue to grab a cup of coffee with Satan and listen to his well-rehearsed rant about how you will never be good enough. We just sit and listen, accepting everything he says as the gospel truth. I am not one to blame everything on Satan; we can also do a number on ourselves. However, Scripture makes it very clear that Satan is the accuser—that he uses our past against us so we will become self-loathing, and therefore impotent in doing things for God. There comes a point when we have to choose to refuse to spend any more time with him and understand that he is not our friend—he does not have our best interest in mind.

Most people try to stay somewhat optimistic, wanting to be positive and to live joyful lives. Other people seem happiest when they are wallowing in their misery! Most of us don't want our friends and family to think we are the poster child for the Doom & Gloom Club, but there are times when we slip into negative, contaminating thought patterns.

Destructive patterns of thinking can and do wreak havoc in our lives. We spend a lot of time recycling our past mistakes. We use ourselves as punching bags by beating ourselves up with thoughts like, "I should have"; "Why didn't I?"; and "If only." We end up should've, could've, would've-ing ourselves into a frenzied state of guilt and depression. We label ourselves with belittling statements such as, "I'm worthless"; "I'm unlovable"; "I will fail."

The more these contaminating thoughts loop in our heads, the more depressed, anxious, and worthless we feel. We ultimately contaminate ourselves.

We see our current situation in a negative light by focusing on what is not happening, what we don't have, thinking life is a drag, and nothing is worth doing. Feelings of resentment and frustration often show up when we have this contaminated mindset. We also tend to contaminate any prospect for a brighter future by telling ourselves things like, "Life is hopeless"; "I'll never be anything"; "I'll never be happy."

I once heard someone say, "Where your thoughts go, your feet will follow."[25] By looping those negative thoughts, who knows down what bleak and meager path our feet will take us?

The Replacement Principle

Over and over again, God's Word tells us that we need to choose certain actions if we want to break old thinking habits. As a matter of fact, these actions apply to any habit that keeps us stuck and prevents us from experiencing God's fullness and His freedom. One of several verses that describes this replacement principle is Ephesians 4:21-24:

> Since you have heard about Jesus and have learned the truth that comes from him, throw off your old sinful nature and your former way of life, which is corrupted by lust and deception. Instead, let the Spirit renew your thoughts and attitudes. Put on your new nature, created to be like God—truly righteous and holy (NLT).

---

[25] Author unknown.

These action-oriented verses tell us to do three things: throw off, renew, and put on. We, as children of God, are to throw off our former sinful ways of living. We are then told to renew our minds with Biblical truth. Finally, we are to put on our new nature, a new way of thinking and living. Putting on, renewing, and throwing off are verbs. These are purposeful commands we must act on in order to achieve long-term change.

The Change Process

While *putting off* and *putting on* speak of the external, the verb *renew* calls our attention to the internal. "Be renewed in the spirit of your mind" (Ephesians 4:23 KJV). This is the starting point, the birthplace of our attitudes and our motives. This is what directly influences our external world: our actions and reactions, our behavior and speech, our decisions and the choices we make, all start with the spirit of our mind.

When I start to see myself and others from a God-honoring perspective, I am more likely to put off the old way of doing things, which often leads to sinful tendencies. I then can put on new a behavior that reflects biblical principles for living.

The process of change takes effort on our part. To stop harmful patterns with our thoughts and behaviors, we must purposefully start lining up our thinking with God's Word to put off the old harmful behaviors and put on a new way of doing life. When we do this, lasting change starts from the inside out.

Romans 12:1–2 in *The Message* talks about the replacement principle from a little different slant:

> So here's what I want you to do, God helping you: Take your everyday, ordinary life—your sleeping, eating, going-to-work, and walking-around life—and

place it before God as an offering. Embracing what God does for you is the best thing you can do for him. Don't become so well-adjusted to your culture that you fit into it without even thinking. Instead, fix your attention on God. You'll be changed from the inside out. Readily recognize what he wants from you, and quickly respond to it. Unlike the culture around you, always dragging you down to its level of immaturity, God brings the best out of you, develops well-formed maturity in you.

We start with the renewing of our thoughts. Once we start aligning our thoughts with the truth in God's Word, we then will have a paradigm shift. When I see what I'm doing from God's perspective, it helps me put off my old, sinful behaviors and put on new behaviors. These new behaviors reflect the renewed mind, which is now changed by God's truth. This is what our pattern starts to look like:

Renewed mind + putting off old harmful patterns + replacing them by putting on biblical patterns = Freedom, peace, joy

Example:
Renewed mind: "I am a child of God who is loved and provided for." + Putting off: any stealing behavior (taking things that do not belong to me or getting things through deception or manipulation) + Putting on: "I am now a habitual worker for God's kingdom as a gift giver!"

The replacement principle is difficult to do. However, when we are consistent, the work we put in enables us to operate and live in the way God is calling us to.

Stay Calm

When Israel finally left Egypt after many years of captivity, Pharaoh had a change of heart about letting them go, so he sent his army and their chariots to bring the Israelites back to Egypt.

When Israel saw that the Egyptians were about to overtake them, they panicked and then jumped all over Moses saying, "Why did you bring us out here to die in the wilderness? Weren't there enough graves for us in Egypt? What have you done to us? Why did you make us leave Egypt?" (Exodus 14:11 NLT).

They were stressing out, to say the least. I love Moses's response to them in verse 14. Moses said, "The Lord himself will fight for you. Just stay calm" (NLT). And then God replied to Moses, "Why are you crying out to me? Tell the people to get moving! Pick up your staff and raise your hand over the sea. Divide the water so that the Israelites can walk through the middle of the sea on dry ground" (verses 15-16 NLT).

They were to *renew* their thoughts with the knowledge that it was not up to them to fight the Egyptians, but God Himself was going to fight on their behalf. They were also to *put off* their worry and panic so that God's peace could come in. They were then to *put on* taking action that reflects God's truth. They got up and moved, and they let God do what only God could do!

I know there are times when we feel so beat up and so overwhelmed by the struggles we face that it seems like it's all we can do just to get out of bed in the morning. We look at what is about to overtake us. We can hardly breathe for the weight we are carrying. I know. I have been there myself. But according to God's Word, we were not designed to carry all our worries. God wants us to give them over to Him.

This is where the putting or casting off comes in—to cast off the old and renew our minds with God's promises and to put that truth on! This means that every time Satan comes knocking at the door of your mind, wanting you to come and hang out with him, you answer his call immediately with God's truth about the issue you are facing and allow the peace of God to take hold.

It's important for you to remember that you must be consistent in doing this! Behind every storm is a spiritual battle! I have noticed that it seems behind every issue we face is a spiritual battle. I have seen this not only in my practice in working with people who are dealing with major situations, but also in my own life. Let me explain. It is easy for me to tell somebody that God can provide for all their needs when my bank account is full. It is also easy for me to share with sick people about God's healing hand when I am healthy. It's in the difficult times that I need to stick with it and be consistent and determined to renew my mind, put off the old, and put on the new. When I face the spiritual issues behind my difficulties, that is when my faith-walk begins.

The difficulties we face in life can show us where we are in our faith-walk. If we are dealing with financial issues, the spiritual battle could be trust. Is God really going to provide for my needs as He said He would? Do I have faith that He will come through for me? If we are dealing with jealousy, our spiritual battle could be discontentment. Why won't God provide me with a better job like his? When will God bring along someone for me to spend my life with like them? We are bombarded with destructive thoughts about the issue we are facing. This is when we need to renew our minds in God's truth, get rid of these destructive thoughts, and replace them with new thoughts. "God does care. He will walk me through this financial situation. I will rely on Him through it all." And, "God loves me, and He has given me so many blessings. I have a job, a place to sleep, and food to eat. He has my life planned out for me, and He will continue to bless me with good things. I just need to look for them."

When we are dealing with any issues or storms in our lives, we need to choose to *put off* anything that will keep us stuck or hinder our walks with God. We need to *renew* our minds with thoughts from God's Word. We need to use these thoughts to help us *put on* new attitudes and mindsets. We will then move forward and behave in ways that glorify God. When we see the result of switching out our bad habits with truly renewing habits from God's Word, we see why and how to stop having coffee with Satan!

CHAPTER EIGHT

Thought Ingredients That Spoil the Recipe

Your imagination has much to do with your life . . . It is for you to decide how you want your imagination to serve you.

—*Philip Conley*

One Sunday after church, I had the idea that I would make southern-fried chicken for my family. The problem was that I had never made it before, so I went online to find a recipe. I finally found a recipe by a pleasant looking lady with large, white hair who looked like anything she made would be wonderful.

I downloaded the recipe, and off I went on my southern-fried quest. I got the chicken and all the other ingredients—the buttermilk, flour, pepper, and other spices—adding and mixing the ingredients as I went. When I looked at the recipe to see how much salt to use, it told me use two cups of salt. Okay, this sounded good; I like a lot of seasoning in my food. I rolled the chicken in the flour concoction and put the pieces in the hot oil. The smell of the frying chicken was permeating the whole house, and it smelled good. Even my wife and kids were coming to me asking when it would be done. The smell of the chicken was making them hungry. To tell you the truth, I was also getting impatient to eat.

My stomach was growling so loudly that it sounded like we were in the middle of a thunderstorm.

Finally, everything was ready. I had made biscuits, green beans, mashed potatoes, and my fried chicken. I piled all our plates high with chicken and my other sides. While I served it up, I played out a scenario in my mind, imagining the reactions of my family after they took a bite of *Dad's Famous Chicken*. They would turn to me with a rapturous look on their face and say,*"This is the best chicken we have ever eaten! You're the greatest, Dad!"*

This was where fantasy and reality collided—that moment when your expectations of a situation and what actually happens look nothing alike. I can't remember who took the first bite of what we now call the *Dead Sea Chicken*, but it was not pleasant. If my family members could have spit the chicken out, they would have. But because of the enormous amount of salt they had just bitten into, their mouths instantly dried up. They had no more water in their bodies to do the job, so all they could do was just let it drop out of their mouths and onto their plates.

My wife, with a drawn face, said, "Oh honey, we can't eat this. How much salt did you use?"

The first thing I said was, "It's not my fault! I followed the big-haired lady's recipe I found on the internet to the letter, and it said to use two cups of salt."

"Let me see the recipe," was all she said. Sure enough, the recipe said two cups. "This has to be a misprint," Kathy said.

I pointed to the recipe. "See? I told you. I told you! I followed the recipe to the letter." We found out later that it was a typo.

It is amazing how too much of any one ingredient can ruin the entire recipe. That single ingredient can contaminate the other ingredients in a way that causes the entire recipe to be inedible, causing ourselves and others to miss out on a good experience.

The same goes for our life recipes. There are some spoiler

ingredients that can affect your recipe in a way that produces a bitter outcome for not only you, but others around you as well. These spoiler ingredients reside in our thoughts and in our attitudes.

Charles R. Woodson says, "The important and decisive factor in life is not what happens to us, but the attitude we take toward what happens. The surest revelation of one's character is the way one bears one's suffering. Circumstances and situations may color life, but by the grace of God, we have been given the power to choose what that color shall be. The effect that misfortune, handicap, sickness, and sorrow have upon life is determined by the way in which we meet them."[26] Our beliefs and views of the world, not our circumstances, determine our emotions, feelings, and behaviors. Epictetus, a Greek philosopher who lived 2000 years ago (about 55-135 AD) said, "People are disturbed not by things, but by the views which they take of them."[27] What I tell myself about any situation, directly influences how that situation affects me.

There are a number of thought ingredients and attitude ingredients in a life recipe that play major roles in producing a toxic, stress-laden life. You may identify with one or more of these ingredients in your life's recipes. They are blame shifting, catastrophizing, can't-stand-its, what-ifs, over-generalizing, assuming, shoulds and musts, all-or-nothing, comparing, perfectionism, labeling, and taking everything as a personal attack. Let's take a closer look at each ingredient and how it affects our recipes.

Blame Shifting

Norman Cousins says, "A human being fashions his consequences as surely as he fashions his goods or his dwelling. Nothing that he

---

[26] http://www.quoteswise.com/zig-ziglar-quotes-5.html

[27] https://www.brainyquote.com/quotes/epictetus_104206

says, thinks or does is without consequences."[28] A characteristic highly successful people possess is that they take ownership of their actions and their outcomes by being proactive. If they are not getting the results they want, there is no blaming or giving up. Like a good cook, they simply tweak the ingredients in their life recipe until they get the desired results.

So often we say to ourselves, "I will be happy once this person does this or that"; "When I get to a certain stage in my life I will . . ."; or "If everything aligns just right, my life will turn out great." Those people who make a difference, in others and in their own lives, don't wait on someone or something external to change them or their situations. They make the changes themselves.

More often than not, we tend to blame-shift when things don't turn out right. We blame others for all the problems we are experiencing in our lives and why we can't get past the obstacles we are dealing with. This behavior is nothing new; it's been going on since time began. Adam and Eve tried to shift blame for the notorious apple incident. Genesis 3:12-13 gives the account of the blame-shifting: "The man said, 'The woman you put here with me—she gave me some fruit from the tree, and I ate it.' Then the LORD God said to the woman, 'What is this you have done?' The woman said, 'The serpent deceived me, and I ate.'"

Adam, trying to cover his behind, started off not only blaming Eve for giving him the fruit and making him eat it, but he also had the nerve to blame God for putting the temptress there in the first place! If she had not been there, he wouldn't have sinned. The woman then said, "The devil made me do it." No one took ownership for their role in what happened, but instead they blame-shifted.

It's also not uncommon for us to blame God (as Adam did) for the recipes we have been following. Proverbs 19:3 says, "A person's

---

[28] https://www.brainyquote.com/quotes/norman_cousins_156508

own folly leads to their ruin, yet their heart rages against the LORD." We do things we know we have no business doing in the first place. Our actions are either hurting others or going against God's Word. Other times we know what God is calling us to do, and we are not doing it and are living in disobedience. The problems and pain that are associated with our actions show up in our emotions or relationships. That's when we shift the blame to God for the negative outcomes that come from our own bad behavior.

One of the best things we could do for ourselves when dealing with issues is to lose interest in finding fault. Often, we end up spending more time finding someone to point our finger at than we do trying to find the solution to our problem. The ingredient of blame-shifting not only contaminates your recipe, but it also keeps you stuck.

Catastrophizing

We catastrophize a situation or event when we make it worse in our minds than it really is. We make a mountain out of a molehill, or we spend $10 on a ten-cent problem. When we're stuck behind a slow driver, our tendency would be to make it worse than it really is by thinking, "This is terrible! I can't believe this is happening to me! This is the worst thing that could happen right now!" An alternative way of thinking would be to ask yourself, "Is this situation really a catastrophe or just an inconvenience? Will I remember this tomorrow? Will the world come to an end? Chances are, it probably won't, and it's just an inconvenience."

Can't-Stand-Its

These are the things in life that happen that are a hassle or an inconvenience that annoys us. Our thoughts go from not liking the situation and being annoyed to, "I can't stand it!" We need to differentiate between being annoyed or not liking something and feeling like we can't stand something or someone. We can ask ourselves, "Does this line of thinking help in any way or make things worse?"

What-Ifs

An endless list of bad things can happen in the course of our lives. "What if they don't like me?" "What if I fail?" "What if they think I am stupid, and they laugh at me?"

By what-if-ing, we are projecting the worst-case scenario onto the future event. With this ingredient, we take a negative possibility and turn it into a probability—what could happen will probably now happen. This kind of thinking keeps us paralyzed. We're so focused on what could happen that we miss out on living. Left unchecked or taken to an extreme, it can slip into paranoid thinking.

This quip, ascribed to Mark Twain, says it all: "I am an old man and have known a great many troubles—but most of them never happened."[29]

Over-Generalizing

This involves generalized statements, usually using the words "always," "never," "everyone," and "no one." It is all-or-nothing thinking. While there may be a shred of truth to the statement, it is clearly an overgeneralization like, "Everybody knows I made a bad choice"; "Nobody wants to be around me"; "I always get stuck

---

[29] A version of this quip was ascribed to Mark Twain in a Singapore newspaper in 1923.

behind the slowest driver"; "You never listen to me." Although it's easy to get trapped by this kind of thinking, especially if we're angry or depressed, it's terribly destructive. Over-generalizing clouds our perception of life. We need to catch ourselves when we start thinking like this and redirect our thoughts to less generalized statements. Instead of saying, "You never listen to me," change it to, "There are times when you don't listen to me and it frustrates me."

Assuming

"This is what they're probably thinking about me." "Their real motive is . . ." "They did that on purpose!" "The world's out to get me." We project onto others what we think they're thinking, what we think their motives are, and what we think they're feeling, and most of the time we are wrong. This is a surefire way to cause emotional distress in ourselves and our relationships. When we assume, it is almost always negative; very rarely do we have positive assumptions. That means when we mind-read, it will be negative. When we jump to conclusions, they too will be negative. An effective way to deal with assumptions is by separating fact from fiction. If it's based on fact, then I will deal with it—if it's based on assumptions, I will ignore it.

Shoulds and Musts

This thought distortion focuses on the absolute demands we make on ourselves, on the world, and on others. "I should"; "The world should"; and "They should." There is a connection between the "shoulds" we tell ourselves and some of the negative emotions we feel. "I should" promotes unrealistic expectations and feelings of guilt and insecurities in us. The general feeling that the world should do something about your circumstance cultivates resentment. When we focus on the phrase, "they should," we become angry.

Other "should" words are must, must not, and ought to. If we are not careful, we can end up stepping into a big pile of "shoulds." When we find ourselves with "should" thinking taking over, we change them over to statements like, "It would be nice if they would . . ."; "It would have been better if my circumstance were different"; "It's not really what I was after, but it will be okay." By changing the "should" to other statements that are not focused on absolutes, we free ourselves from this maddening cycle.

All-or-Nothing

If you don't do things just right or come in first in whatever you are doing, you see yourself as a failure. Or when you do something good and receive ninety-nine "attaboys" and one negative comment, you end up focusing on the one negative, totally ignoring the ninety-nine positives. We can live in all-or-nothing thinking for ourselves and for others as well, holding them to an impossible standard and making life miserable for all. The best thing we can do is to show compassion to ourselves and others by not discounting all the good because it did not end perfectly.

Perfectionism

A close cousin to the all-or-nothing ingredient is the, "I have to be perfect" ingredient. If what I am doing is not done perfectly, then it's not any good and I am a failure. Often with this ingredient, we struggle with feelings of insecurity that sound like, "I'm not good enough," or "I have to perform at a certain level to be accepted." We end up falling into a performance trap.

We can do several things to counter this negative ingredient.

First, we need to understand that perfection is a subjective perspective, meaning you only see things from your perspective instead of looking at things objectively. But what is perfect for you might not be perfect for me, hence there is no agreed upon standard for us to even measure whether something is perfect. It's all a matter of opinion. You could say a certain work of art is perfect, that it is a masterpiece. I might say you are nuts—it's a piece of junk. We all see things differently.

Second, we need to tell ourselves that we will do our best at whatever we do instead of having to do everything perfectly. One of the best things we can do for ourselves is to show ourselves compassion. The only perfect person I know of lived over two thousand years ago, and I am not Him.

Comparing

It is tempting and oh so easy to compare ourselves to others. However, when we compare, we compare our weaknesses to someone else's strengths. I have a good friend who has run a number of marathons. I can't even drive the distance of a marathon without stopping along the way to use the bathroom, let alone run a marathon. I am not built to haul my two-hundred-forty-pound carcass twenty-six miles. However, I can lift weights with the best of them or run three miles and feel good. If I start comparing my inability to run a marathon with my friend's ability to run several marathons a year, I start feeling like a failure. I start telling myself, "I must be in awful shape."

We can also do this to others in our lives, especially our loved ones. We can compare our spouse to our friend's spouse, or we can compare our children to the other kids at school or church. I once heard that the fastest way for a church to die is to compare itself with another church. Comparing is one of the quickest paths to discontentment, failing to thank God for the uniqueness and gifts He gave us or our family members. One of the best things we can do for the comparing bug is to live with a grateful spirit for what we do have.

Labeling

Labeling is calling myself names when the events in my life don't go the way I want them to. I make self-defacing statements such as, "I'm an idiot"; "Failure!"; "Loser!"; "I will never be good enough"; and "I am a royal mess-up!" We can also label others if they don't do what we are asking them to do or do not meet our expectations: "You slob"; "You are so stupid, you don't have a clue about anything"; "That guy is a numbskull"; and "You're worthless." When it comes to dealing with others, I like what Dale Carnegie said: "When dealing with people, remember you are not dealing with creatures of logic, but creatures of emotion."[30] When we label others, we can end up emotionally maiming someone for life. When we label ourselves, we create in ourselves a sense of worthlessness. So stop labeling! It's verbal assassination.

Ask yourself what your relationships would look like if you spent more time looking for the positives instead of focusing on the negatives, because the direction you are looking affects the direction you go. When I was a kid and my dad was driving, he would take his eyes off the road to look at something out the passenger window and the vehicle would go the direction he was looking. This slight veering scared everyone in the car! The same holds true for us. We are going to go the direction we are looking. If we are in the habit of thinking negatively toward ourselves or others, then our days, weeks, or even months are going to go in a

---

[30] https://www.brainyquote.com/quotes/dale_carnegie_130727

negative direction. But if we can get into the habit of turning our minds the other way and thinking positively, guess what? Our days, weeks, and months are going to be positive. It's all in the direction we are thinking.

Taking Everything as a Personal Attack

In this way of thinking, if others don't happen to do what we want them to do, we take it as an assault on ourselves. If they don't meet our expectations, they must be doing so to get back at us, or they are trying to sabotage what we are trying to do. Whatever the underlying motive, it was done "on purpose" and it was about us.

By taking everything as a personal attack, we are also assuming. We are assuming that they are out to get us or planning to undermine what we are doing. In essence, we are making it all about us, when we are probably the furthest thing from their mind.

A little girl was walking along a path to her grandfather's house on a cold January morning. Along the way, she came upon a snake curled up, half-frozen on the path in front of her. The little girl took pity on the snake, picked it up, and put it under her coat to get warm. She continued down the path, but not long after she put the creature under her coat, she felt an intense pain. She opened her coat up, and to her surprise, she found the snake biting into her side. She pulled it off, threw it down, and cried out, "Why did you bite me? I was trying to help you! Why did you do it?" The snake simply looked up at the little girl and said, "You knew what I was when you picked me up."

If we continue to use these contaminated ingredients toward ourselves and others, we shouldn't be surprised when we get bit. Just like the snake, it's in their nature to strike and do as much damage as they can. And it is up to us to stop showing them pity by justifying why we hold on to them.

Read through the list of bad recipe ingredients below. Which ones can you relate to? Check every ingredient you struggle with, then take several minutes to pray and ask God to help you get rid of these ingredients. For each ingredient you checked, ask God to reveal how you can counter it and jot it down next to the ingredient. Pray every morning and ask God to help you to do this. When you mess up, ask God to forgive you, learn from it, and keep going.

- Blame-shifting
- Catastrophizing
- Can't-stand-its
- What-ifs
- Over-generalizing
- Assuming
- Shoulds and musts
- All-or-nothing
- Comparing
- Perfectionism
- Labeling
- Taking everything as a personal attack

It is not until we remove these kinds of thoughts that we, and those around us, can experience relief from them.

CHAPTER NINE

Bad Life Recipes

We design our lives through the power of choices.
—Richard Bach

Recipe, according to the Encarta Dictionary is "a method of doing something or a combination of circumstances likely to bring something about," or "a list of ingredients and instructions for making something, especially a food dish."

Traditions can play an important part in the makeup of our families. You can probably recall, and even have fond memories of, the special family traditions during occasions such as birthday celebrations, summer vacations, holidays, or even bedtime rituals. Maybe you are starting new traditions in your family that you hope can be played out in generations to come. Whatever the case, the traditions we choose to follow are the things we often remember the most. They can also have a direct influence on our life.

Our Outcomes Reflect Our Actions

Second Peter 1:2 reads, "Grace and peace be yours in abundance through the knowledge of God and of Jesus our Lord." In reading this, we see that grace and peace are by-products of our knowledge of God and of our Lord Jesus. The more we know God and His character and who we are in Christ Jesus, the more grace, peace, and joy increase. They are by-products of our actions.

How many people do you know who say, "I want to find peace in my life?" They can look long and hard and never find it, because peace is a by-product. It's not until we do certain actions that we find peace.

This goes both ways. If we use bad ingredients, we create bad life recipes. The by-products of these recipes are stress, negativity, and misery. Let's take a look at a bad recipe:

My Recipe for Ruining My Day Without Really Trying

- I will plan to do twice as much as I can realistically accomplish. Over-scheduling is the easiest way to drive myself crazy.
- I will be inflexible. Demanding that everyone do things my way is guaranteed to raise my blood pressure.
- I will demand perfection in myself and others, that way I have earned the right to be miserable when something goes wrong.
- I will worry about anything and everything, even those things over which I have no control.
- I will take everything as a personal attack. I assume any mistake is aimed at me.
- I will leave my sense of humor at home. I will treat everything, no matter how minor, as a matter of life or death.
- I will avoid doing what I know needs to be done. Procrastination is a great ingredient for producing guilt.
- I will tell myself that there is absolutely nothing I can do about the anger, anxiety, unhappiness, or depression I am experiencing. My feelings are caused by what happens to me.

- I will tell myself that I must please everyone. It is necessary to be approved and loved by everyone.
- I will assume everything. My actions are based on assumptions.
- I will live in the past or in the future, forgetting about today.
- I will not keep my words impeccable. Gossip, lies, and sarcasm will be served on my daily menu.
- I will take God out of my day. Things will be done my way, not His.

Blend ingredients thoroughly. Bake on high for twenty-four hours, waking throughout the night to stir ingredients every few hours. Let simmer for several more hours. Serve dish hot and enjoy!

Proverbs 16:25 says, "There is a way that seems right to a man, but its end is the way of death" (NKJV). When we follow a recipe for our life that has unhealthy or destructive ingredients (as illustrated in the above example), the natural by-product of our action will be internal and external distress. We might want to have peace and not experience stress in our lives, but if we don't change the way we are handling things, we will be unable to change the outcome. Galatians 6:7 says, "Do not be deceived: God cannot be mocked. A man reaps what he sows."

Engrained Recipes

We have used some recipes for such a long time that we don't even need to look at the recipe card anymore in order to make a certain dish. One of my father-in-law's favorite pies his mother made when he was child was called meal pie. One of the ingredients was cornmeal. After he got married, my mother-in-law wanted to make meal pie for him. She asked his mother repeatedly for the recipe, but she couldn't give it to her because it was an unwritten recipe. In order to get the recipe, she had to watch her mother-in-law make this pie repeatedly, writing down every step she made. She finally got the recipe!

We tend to do the same thing in our lives. There are actions, belief systems, and thought processes we do repeatedly, because it's what we learned at an early age by watching or being influenced by others (usually someone of significance). Good or bad, right or wrong, we follow those engrained recipes. We need to start evaluating our recipes to determine if they are destructive and hindering us from achieving our full potential or if they are indeed healthy recipes. You can tell the difference by the outcome of the recipe. Does it create stress? Do I feel less than? Is it destructive to relationships?

One example of an engrained recipe is emotional eating, which stems from the basic areas of insecurity and fear. Something or someone will trigger an uncomfortable emotion, and the person eats in order to soothe that feeling. They do this repeatedly every time they feel that emotion, and it becomes engrained. The negative outcome of this engrained recipe, however, is that this person will usually wind up gaining weight, which perpetuates negative self-talk and self-image. Let's look at one person's recipe:

Susan's One-Week Recipe for Emotional Eating[31]

- Monday: Husband out-of-town this week—go out to eat so the time passes faster
- Tuesday: Busy and emotional day at work—find something to eat to make myself feel better (usually sweets)
- Wednesday: Something good happens—why not celebrate with a meal out?
- Thursday: Come home from work very tired—eat out so I don't have to work in the kitchen—order good, fattening food

---

[31] Some names have been changed to protect privacy.

- Friday: Begin to feel lonely—what better way to help me get out and around people than to go out and eat?
- Saturday: Throw in a home-cooked meal with dessert and polish it off (the sooner it's gone, the quicker I can get on with my weight loss plan on Monday)
- Feel hopeless about myself ever being thin again—eat more to drown out my feelings of disgust
- Realize that my husband thinks my extra fat is unattractive, which drives me to eat more—he should love me unconditionally
- Hear parents and siblings make fun of fat people—boy, does that candy bar taste good!
- Lose all hope that I can gain control of my eating. Forget Monday. I give up!

Generational Recipes

Listen, O Israel! The LORD is our God,
The LORD alone. And you must love
The LORD your God with all your heart,
All your soul, and all your strength.
And you must commit yourselves wholeheartedly
To these commands that I am giving you today.
Repeat them again and again to your children.
Talk about them when you are at home and
When you are on the road, when you are going to bed
And when you are getting up. Tie them to your hands
And wear them on your forehead as reminders.
Write them on the doorposts of your house
And on your gates.
Deuteronomy 6:4-9 NLT

Some recipes are handed down from generation to generation and have been in families for decades, or even centuries! This can be either positive or negative. We can't change the past, but it is within our power to control what we pass on to our kids. We need to ask ourselves what kind of recipes we are handing down to the next generation. It can be a mind-boggling task just to think about this, but we are passing down recipes whether we plan to or not, so why not be deliberate about it? Some people pass down recipes for alcoholism, domestic violence, low self-acceptance, anxiety, depression, and the list goes on. Other people pass down recipes for healthy self-acceptance, boundaries, balanced living, spirituality, how to love and respect a spouse, how to resolve conflict, and many other healthy habits. Good or bad, people will say, "That's just the way we've always done it in our family."

Johnny grew up in a family where praise and approval were based on his performance. If he made straight As, he was praised. If he made the sports team, he was praised. If he scored points, he was praised. But if he didn't perform like his parents thought he should, he was either ignored or reprimanded. Performance-based approval (the basic source of fear and insecurity) was ingrained in him and stuck with him into adulthood. As an adult, he was driven to excel, to reach the top of the corporate ladder.

He had a difficult time in his role as husband and father because he had turned into a workaholic. He could never achieve enough to earn the approval he so desired. Eventually, he began to self-medicate with alcohol because the stress was killing him. The drinking, however, only made things worse. The next thing he knew, he was repeating the same scenarios with his own son. He was caught in a destructive cycle, and he couldn't see a way out. If he kept following the same ingrained recipe, disaster was just around the corner. Johnny knew he had to find a way to rewrite this recipe.

Johnny's Recipe for Attaining Approval

- Be the best and have the best
- Anything less than perfect is not acceptable; it's all-or-nothing
- I will label myself as incompetent or a failure if I don't reach my goal
- I will do whatever it takes to succeed; nothing will stand in my way
- When things get too stressful, I will use alcohol to cope
- I will pass down the same patterns to my children

You will be glad to know that Johnny is now living from new recipe card, and he is doing extremely well. He understood that not only did he have to set new, healthy goals for what he wanted to change, but he also knew he had to be tenaciously intentional in changing and implementing a new set of ingredients that reflected his desired outcomes.

Like Johnny, we need to ask ourselves, "What recipes were handed down to me? Were they positive or negative? Am I choosing to follow those recipes? How are they affecting what I am handing down?" When we identify what was handed down to us and whether it was positive or negative, we need to decide whether we will continue following the recipe or whether we will discard it and replace it with a new one. Once we have done that, we can focus on the recipes we want to hand down.

My parents passed down the recipe pertaining to the phone. Even years later when I was doing well financially, when the phone rang, I got that same old sick feeling I had growing up, thinking the worst. I had to force myself to answer it. It was not until many years later, instead of thinking the worst-case scenario when the phone rang, I told myself that my fears were unwarranted and that I would use the phone ringing to cue me to pray for others.

To a child, what goes on in the home is the norm, even if it's a place of chaos. When they start their own families, they bring their norms, good or bad, into their homes. It has been said that "Children are the living messages we send to a time we will not see."[32] So what messages are we sending?

You can't go back and change the past—neither the things that happened to you or the things you caused. You can, however, change the way in which you deal with those experiences or events. It's time to determine if you have any unhealthy recipes. You can figure out whether a recipe is bad or good by looking at the outcome. This is the time to be completely authentic, not minimizing or denying issues.

In the story of the woman at the well (John 4:16-18), Jesus tells her to go and get her husband. However, she was not married but living with a man. Of course, Jesus knew this and wasn't trying to set her up or make her feel bad. In asking her to get her husband, He wanted her to get completely honest, to get real with where she was. He wants us to do the same! Make a list of those undesirable outcomes to identify one of your unhealthy recipes, and then list the steps in that recipe. You can't change the unhealthy recipe until you identify the steps you are taking.

Take a moment to reflect on the recipes that have been handed down in your family. Which recipes caused strife and stress, such as a recipe for expecting perfection? Which recipes caused joy and peace, like a recipe for experiencing fun and laughter together? Then, take a moment to reflect on the recipes you want to pass on to your children or the people around you. What do you want

---

[32] Neil Postman, *The Disappearance of Childhood*, (Manhattan: Vintage/Random House, 1994)

to foster in your children or your loved ones? How do you want to behave toward them? What generational recipes do you want to pass down? How about a recipe for treating others as you would want to be treated? What new recipes do you want to create? Maybe a recipe for living a life of encouragement? Write them down on the following recipe cards:

My Generational Recipes Passed Down to Me:

-
-
-
-
-
-

My Generational Recipes to Pass Down to Others:

-
-
-
-
-
-

In Deuteronomy 6:4-9, we are told to repeat God's laws, to talk about them, to write them down, to live them out. Our kids and loved ones see us doing a lot of things—they see us reading the paper, doing the dishes, walking the dog, and so on. However, do they see us doing the things that are most important, things they can take with them when they are grown and starting their own families? They need to see us resolving conflicts in a healthy manner, communicating, loving, and respecting one another. We need to be deliberate about these recipes.

Here is an example of an endearing generational recipe. It was written to Ann Landers from a loving daughter about her parents.

A Small Metal Box

> Dear Ann Landers,
>
> Last weekend, we celebrated my parents' 50th wedding anniversary. This morning they left on a long-awaited trip to Hawaii. They were as excited as if it were their honeymoon! When my parents married, they had only enough money for a three-day trip 50 miles from home. They made a pact then that each time they made love, they would put a dollar in a special metal box and save it for a honeymoon in Hawaii for their 50th anniversary. Dad was a policeman, and Mom was a schoolteacher. They lived in a modest house and did all their own repairs. Raising five children was a challenge, and sometimes money was short. But no matter what emergency came up, Dad would not let Mom take any money out of the "Hawaii account." As the amount grew, they put it in a savings account and then bought CDs.
>
> My parents were always very much in love. I can remember Dad coming home and telling Mom, "I have a dollar in my pocket." She would smile at him and reply, "I know just how to spend it." When each of us children married, Mom and Dad gave us a small metal box and told us their secret, which we found enchanting. All five of us are now saving for

our dream honeymoons. Mom and Dad never told us how much money they managed to save, but it must have been considerable because when they cashed in those CD's, they had enough for airfare to Hawaii, plus hotel accommodations for 10 days and plenty of spending money. Before they boarded the plane, Dad winked and said, "Tonight we are starting an account for Cancun. That should only take 25 years!"

Ann, I thought you'd enjoy this story about 50 great years of intimacy in marriage!

—From a loving daughter in Abilene, Texas[33]

--By permission of Esther P. Lederer Trust and Creators Syndicate, Inc

The recipe these loving parents passed down to their children is one full of love, respect, and persistence. What a precious gift they gave to their children—showing what living out love looks like, so their children can model and pass it down to their children. I believe these parents understood that what they did as parents did not just affect them, but it rippled out, touching not only their children, but their children's children as well.

A vital ingredient we need to add when developing and implementing our new generational recipes we want to pass down to our children is making God the main ingredient. Psalm 127:1-2 says, "Unless the LORD builds the house, the work of the builders is wasted. Unless the LORD protects a city, guarding it with sentries will do no good. It is useless for you to work so hard from early

---

[33] http://www.chickensoup.com/book-story/53351/the-metal-box. To find out more about Ann Landers and read her past columns, visit http://www.creators.com/features/classic-ann-landers.

morning until late at night, anxiously working for food to eat; for God gives rest to his loved ones" (NLT).

Go to Him first, asking Him to take control, and guide you in creating your new recipe. Tapping into a power greater than your own ensures that you will have a recipe that reflects God's best for you and the generations to come.

CHAPTER TEN
Replacing Core Ingredients

How does one become a butterfly? You must want to fly so much that you are willing to give up being a caterpillar.

—Trina Paulus

This inscription is written on the tomb of an Anglican Bishop in Westminster Abby: "When I was young and free and my imagination had no limits, I dreamed of changing the world. As I grew older and wiser, I discovered the world would not change, so I shortened my sights somewhat and decided to change only my country. But it, too, seemed immovable. As I grew into my twilight years, in one last desperate attempt, I settled for changing only my family, those closest to me, but alas, they would have none of it. And now as I lie on my deathbed, I suddenly realize: If I had only changed myself first, then by example I would have changed my family. From their inspiration and encouragement, I would then have been able to better my country and, who knows, I may have even changed the world."

Don't wait for others to change your recipe. The longer we wait on others to fix us, without taking any action ourselves, the more our frustration builds. Our frustration, left unchecked, can turn toxic. It can turn into resentment and bitterness toward others whom we feel did not meet our expectations, like our spouse, pastors, friends, God. When we live in this kind of toxic frustration, we take on the victim role.

Victor Frankl, psychiatrist, author, and holocaust survivor wrote: "We, who lived in concentration camps, can remember the men who walked through the huts comforting others, giving away their last piece of bread. They may have been few in number, but they offer sufficient proof that everything can be taken from a man but one thing: the last of human freedoms—to choose one's attitude in any given set of circumstances, to choose one's own way."[34]

It starts with a choice. Those individuals, who were in the concentration camps whom Victor Frankl wrote about, chose amid their dreadful position to take action and minister to those around them. By choosing to do something positive, in a horrible situation, even if it was for that one moment, they lived outside their prison.

William Jennings Bryan wrote, "Destiny is not a matter of chance, it is a matter of choice; it is not a thing to be waited for, it is a thing to be achieved."[35]

Changing How You View Your Old Recipes

We need to change the way we look at our old harmful recipes and the ingredients that make them up. We need to see them for what they truly are: thieves! This is where you become your own CSI investigator, treating your life as a crime scene. We do this by identifying what the old harmful recipes and their patterns, or ingredients, have stolen from us. If one of the ingredients in your

---

[34] https://www.goodreads.com/quotes/40139-we-who-lived-in-concentration-camps-can-remember-the-men
[35] https://www.brainyquote.com/quotes/william_jennings_bryan_389006

old recipe is worry ("I will worry about everything"), what you are robbed of is sleep, peace, joy, and even physical health.

The effects of following old recipes are not benign. In fact, they will infect multiple areas of our lives and the lives of others as well. If an old ingredient in my life's recipe is holding a grudge ("I will keep records of all wrongs done against me"), it not only robs me of emotional health, but also robs me of a healthy relationship with the other person. I create an environment of tension and anxiety, making people feel like they must walk on eggshells. Seeing the harmful recipes and ingredients for what they truly are (thieves), we start to understand that when we continue to follow the unhealthy recipes, we open ourselves and others up to being robbed of our precious possessions that play such a vital role in healthy living.

Our ingredients fall into one of two areas; they are either contributing to our healthy recipe, or they are contaminating it. You can tell the difference between the two by not only the outcomes they produce, but also the feelings you will experience from them.

If our ingredients are contributing to our recipe, then we will feel energized, experiencing peace, joy, and a sense of connection. They help us to attain our goals, and the feelings we get from contributing ingredients will remain even if our circumstances are less than ideal.

If ingredients are contaminating our recipe, we will experience a deficit. We will have deficits in our energy level, peace, joy and that sense of connectedness with others, and our relationship with God will be distant.

Dietrich Bonhoeffer wrote, "If you board the wrong train, it is no use running along the corridor in the other direction."[36] Once we change the way we look at our old harmful patterns of our

---

[36] https://www.brainyquote.com/quotes/dietrich_bonhoeffer_164002

thoughts and behaviors, seeing them for what they are, we can get off the train and stop moving in the wrong direction.

What Is Your Core Ingredient?

Matthew 6:21 says, "For where your treasure is, there your heart will be also." Every recipe has a core ingredient. Whatever we are using as the core ingredient drives the recipe. If I take a pound of ground beef out of the freezer, I hold a core ingredient that will have a direct effect on the outcome of the dish I make. Depending on the recipe I choose, I can wind up with chili, hamburgers, meatloaf, or tacos. I won't wind up with apple pie.

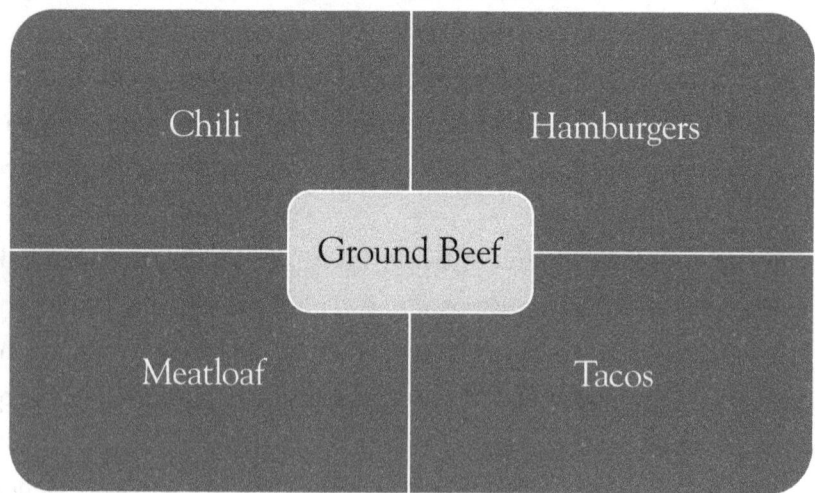

The same goes for our life recipes. We always have a core ingredient that drives the outcome. That ingredient is at the heart of the recipe and majorly influences the entire mixture and ultimately the outcome of our recipe.

A number of things can be our core ingredient: God, self, fear, money, insecurity, possessions, children, work, and so on. Our core ingredient influences and becomes the lens through which we view all the areas of our lives. If fear is our core ingredient, we view the circumstances of our lives from a fearful perspective, promoting a sense of discouragement in us, doubting that we will get through the problems we are facing. A German proverb states, "Fear makes the wolf bigger than he is." Fear breeds in us a pessimistic point of view, making everything seem bigger or worse than it really is. It can cause us to see ourselves in the victim's role, running from a big, vicious, imaginary wolf.

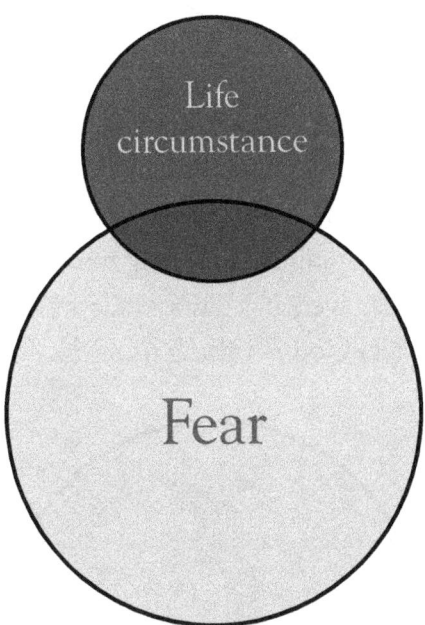

Seeing our relationships from a fearful perspective will often cause us to either avoid intimate relationships altogether, or we will, out of our own insecurities, hold on so tightly to our current relationships that we can end up strangling them, causing that person to feel suffocated. Jealousy is a deadly by-product of fear that can wreak havoc on relationships.

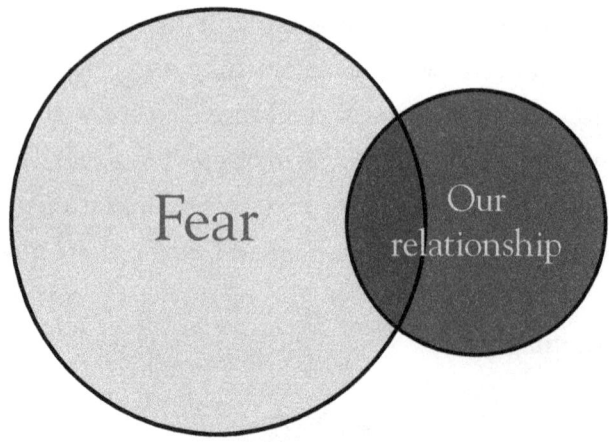

When we are seeing our vocation or ministry from a fearful perspective, we could end up settling for a job or ministry position that we have no passion for and never taking a chance at what we really want. For fear of failure or losing what we do have, we just take what's given us, even if it's not what we really see ourselves doing or what we feel God is calling us to do.

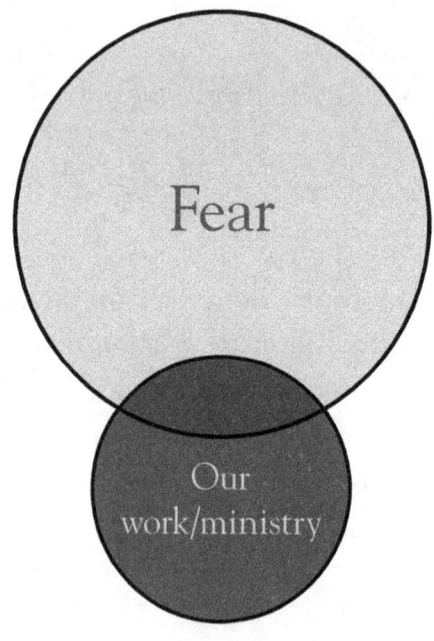

Fear can affect our health in a variety of ways. It can cause us to have sleepless nights. It can cause us to feel depressed or anxious. It can make us more prone to infection and disease. It can paralyze us in every area of our lives.

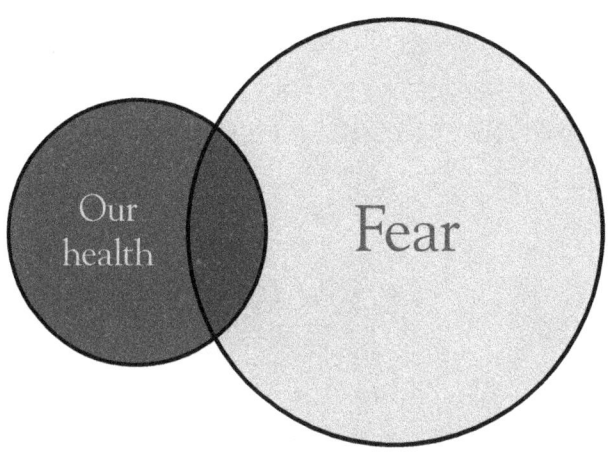

We can make any number of things our core ingredient. Some of these things are even good and healthy in and of themselves. However, when we make them the center of our lives and give them an unhealthy importance, we will have unhealthy lives and see everything through the lenses of an inappropriate core ingredient.

If self is our core ingredient, we will have a self-centered approach to these areas of our lives. If money is our core ingredient, it will take precedence over the people in our lives and even God. If work is our core ingredient, we will spend most of our time pounding the hammer or pounding the computer keyboard. However, if God is our core ingredient, He will influence all the areas of our lives. If ground beef is the core ingredient of a recipe, you won't wind up with apple pie. The same principle applies here: If self is the core ingredient, you won't wind up with godly relationships. If God is the center, your relationships will honor Him. The core ingredient directly affects the outcome.

Matthew 6:33 says, "But seek first his kingdom and his righteousness, and all these things will be given to you as well." This verse shows clearly what our core ingredient should be. Seek God first. Not money, not yourself, not your fears—God. If you are centered on Him, everything else will be about Him too, and He will guide your life. If you choose to center your life on something else, you will not experience the richness, the peace, and joy that God brings to a child centered on Him.

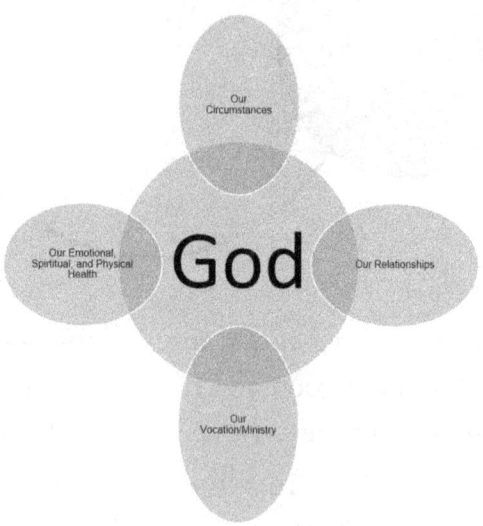

Sydney J. Harris writes, "Ninety percent of the world's woe comes from people not knowing themselves, their abilities, their frailties, and even their real virtues. Most of us go almost all the way through life as complete strangers to ourselves."[37] The question we all need to ask ourselves is, "What is my core ingredient that influences all the areas of my life?" Our core ingredient is what gets us up in the morning and drives our behavior.

Take a few minutes to think and pray about what your core

---

[37] http://thinkexist.com/quotation/ninety_percent_of_the_worlds_woe_comes_from/14844.html

ingredient is. Ask God to reveal what your life is centered on and write it below.

My core ingredient: _____

Is your core ingredient what you want it to be? If not, identify what you want your core ingredient to be and what areas you want it to influence.

What I want my core ingredient to be: _____

What areas I want my core ingredient to influence: _____

_____

_____

_____

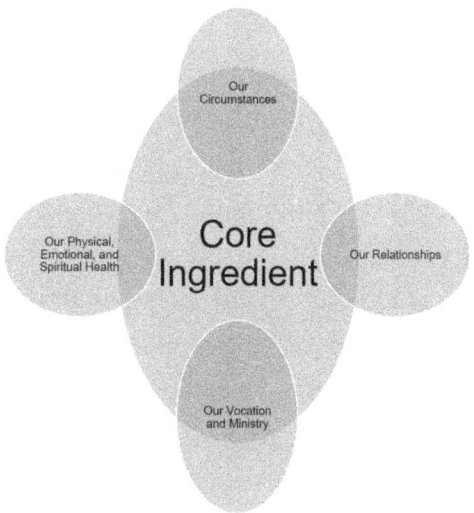

God Blesses Actions Not Intentions

"Then the LORD said to Moses, 'Why are you crying out to me? Tell the Israelites to get up and move'" (Exodus 14:15).

I had a conversation with my dad about a year before he died at the age of ninety-one. It started off as usual with a lot of small talk, but then it took an unexpected turn, at least for me anyway. Dad looked at me and said, "Rick, it's hard getting old. I can't do half the things I once was able to do . . . and I can't remember the other half. But I think the worst thing about getting old is living with regrets. It's the things I knew I was supposed to do and yet didn't that I keep on thinking about. Rick, I sure wish I could do some things differently."

We intend to do all kinds of good things in life. We intend to finish our education, take the family on that trip we have been talking about, tell a family member we love them, forgive the person who hurt us, or ask for forgiveness for hurting someone we love. We can all come up with our own list of what we intended to do but never took the time to do. The question, however, is what we are going to do now with our intentions? Personally, I don't want to be haunted in my older age by the things I intended to do.

Curtis Grant writes, "Having the world's best idea will do you no good unless you act on it. People who want milk shouldn't sit on a stool in the middle of a field in hopes that a cow will back up to them."[38] In studying God's word, I found that God blesses action not intentions. I cannot recall ever coming across a passage where God blessed someone's intentions. However, there is a direct correlation between God-inspired actions and blessing. Before any blessings showed up, there was an action. Just look at Matthew 7:7: "Ask and it will be given to you; seek and you will find; knock and the door will be opened to you." All the verbs in this verse are actions that we take. Ask, seek, knock. This is also true for the many people who worked with God in the Bible as well. If you would like to look some of them up, here is a sampling:

---

[38] http://www.quotes.net/quote/13466

- Joshua and the priests carrying the ark across the Jordan—Joshua 3
- Joshua and the walls of Jericho—Joshua 5:13–6:27
- Gideon overcoming his fears—Judges 6-7
- Nehemiah and the rebuilding of the wall—the book of Nehemiah
- Peter walking on water—Matthew 14:25-33
- Peter healing a lame beggar—Acts 3:1-9

Don't Leave Your Recipe Cards Empty

A behavioral rule of thumb says if you take something away, you have to replace it with something. Matthew 12:43-45 says, "When an impure spirit comes out of a person, it goes through arid places seeking rest and does not find it. Then it says, 'I will return to the house I left.' When it arrives, it finds the house unoccupied, swept clean and put in order. Then it goes and takes with it seven other spirits more wicked than itself, and they go in and live there. And the final condition of that person is worse than the first. That is how it will be with this wicked generation."

If you remove an unhealthy ingredient from your recipe, but don't replace it with a healthy ingredient, the same unhealthy ingredient, or another one, will fill the gap back in. This defeats the purpose of removing the unhealthy ingredient! For example, if I have a habit of thinking I'm inferior, I can't just stop thinking negatively about myself. Stopping the thought is not enough. I have to replace the negative with positive. I need to switch out, "I'm not good enough" with, "God loves me just the way I am, and He will equip me to do what He is asking of me." Or if I have a habit of eating when I'm stressed, instead of just stopping myself from walking to the refrigerator, I can go for a walk or some other activity instead. Otherwise, if I'm not exchanging stress eating with something else, I may lose my will and go to the fridge anyway. I have to replace the negative, whether thought or action, with positive. This is where the process breaks down for a lot of people. They remove the unhealthy ingredient and stop there, and eventually it comes back. It is important not only to remove the unhealthy ingredient, but to replace it with a healthy ingredient.

The Thought Results Cycle

Before we go any further in changing our recipe, we need to review a very important cycle that we go through hundreds of times through the course of the day in all the situations we face. As we learned in chapter 6, the thought results cycle (shown below) affects everything we do. If we want to change the outcomes that are keeping us bogged down, we need to get a handle on the following cycle.

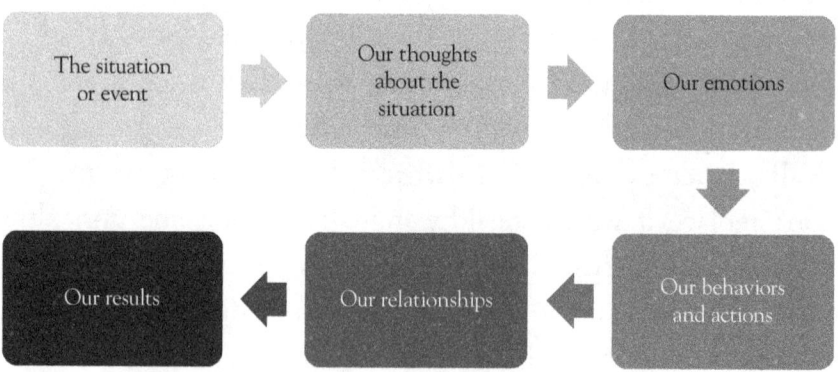

The illustration shown above represents the cycle or pattern we tend to follow. This is how it happens: a situation or event occurs, and it triggers internal dialogue or thoughts. These thoughts and beliefs then determine our behaviors and actions, which influence our interactions and relationships, which determine our results.

Much of the time, when we want to change our results, we

focus on changing our actions. This may work temporarily, but in order to create a lasting change, we need to go to the source of the problem and work on changing our internal dialogue and thoughts.

Let's say one of my beliefs is, "I am the dad, and I am in control. They must do it my way!" What situation might trigger this pattern of thinking that drives my behavior and actions? A trigger could be when one of my kids challenges my authority. When that happens, the internal dialog begins, and my actions mirror that of a drill sergeant. My actions will strain and harm my relationship with my child. The result is a conflicted or even non-existent relationship with my child.

Now, let's say I recognize this destructive behavior and decide I'm going to be nicer and more understanding with my kids, so I focus on changing my actions. This will work until one of my kids challenges me again. Again, the internal dialog will strike up, and the pattern repeats itself. What I need to do is change the internal dialog, the belief system, the old recipe.

To do this, the first thing I need to do is identify the internal dialog. In this case, it's the thought pattern of "I'm the dad, I'm in control, and they must do it my way!" This is a very rigid thought pattern with no room for negotiation.

The second step is to challenge the thought pattern. "I am still the dad, but must it be my way all the time? I need to choose my battles," I tell myself. "What I want is a healthy relationship with my children, so the relationship needs to hold a higher value in my heart than my rigid thinking. I don't have to be a drill sergeant to be in control." These new beliefs will soften my actions and interactions with my kids and result in a better relationship with them.

The Removal of Harmful Ingredients

An important aspect of rewriting our life's recipes is removing harmful ingredients and replacing them with ingredients that create a healthy recipe. We do this by replacing the harmful mistruths we so easily believe with God's truth about who we are and about the situations we are going through. John 8:32 says, "You shall know the truth, and the truth shall make you free" (NKJV). God's truth sets us free from the lies Satan uses to keep us in bondage. We must understand that spiritual warfare is taking place (Ephesians 6:12).

God has a plan for your life, and so does Satan! Satan knows he can't have your soul, so he is going to try to rob you of your peace, your joy, your relationships, your outlook, and anything else he can, so he can leave you impotent to serve God. He does this by influencing your thoughts through distortions and lies. Understand this: Satan is a liar—there is no truth found in him. In fact, he is the father of lies (John 8:44). He is a thief who comes to steal, kill, and destroy!

Have you ever been around a schoolyard bully? They look for anything different or out of the ordinary in order to find their prey. Maybe a nose or ears that happen to be too large, or maybe a kid's pants are a little too short, or maybe they are shy. It doesn't matter what stands out, it's all bait for the bully. They look for anything to use against a child, teasing them often to the point of tears. They tease to get a certain response from their victims, such as running away, avoiding or hiding from the bully, sometimes refusing to go out to the playground for fear they will run into them.

Satan is like a schoolyard bully; he looks for your Achilles heel, zones in on it, and uses it as a weapon against you. An Achilles heel can be your past (regrets, what ifs, traumatic experiences), guilt (half-truths that belittle you), insecurity, ("I am not good enough"; "I am inadequate"; "I am less than"), and fear (fear of failure, fear of success, fear of the "what ifs"). He uses it all because he knows that whatever we are thinking about at any moment owns us. He also knows that if he can influence our thoughts, he can influence us. Whatever he uses, he uses to get a response from us.

God tells us what we need to do when we confront Satan's lies. Second Corinthians 10:3-5 says, "We are human, but we don't wage war as humans do. We use God's mighty weapons, not worldly weapons, to knock down the strongholds of human reasoning and to destroy false arguments. We destroy every proud obstacle that keeps people from knowing God. We capture their rebellious thoughts and teach them to obey Christ" (NLT). So, here's what we need to do to be on the offense instead of listening to Satan's lies.

Offensive Battling

1. Take captive the thought; don't allow yourself to play it over and over in your head. If need be, tell yourself forcefully, "STOP!" This puts a pause on repetitive thoughts.
2. Challenge the lie with God's truth. "If Satan is a liar, then the opposite of what he's telling me must be true. If he says I'm a loser, then God's truth is that I'm more than a conqueror, that I'm of tremendous value to God." Instead of buying into what Satan is selling you, challenge it by recognizing that everything that comes out of Satan's mouth is nothing but deceit.
3. Get God's truth in your head and heart. Write down God's truths about your circumstances. I've included many lists of Scriptures in this book. Use them or other Scriptures that speak the opposite of what Satan is telling you. Memorize what God says about you, confess it, stand firm on it! Thank God for His truth and get real with Him about your struggles. Standing on God's truth will enable you to look at your struggles, not based on who you are, but in relation to who God is. Ephesians 6:10 says, "Be strong in the Lord and in his mighty power."

4. Use God's Word as your Sword of Truth. In Matthew 4:1-11, when Jesus was led into the wilderness to be tempted by Satan, and Satan used lies to tempt Jesus, saying, "If you are the Son of God, tell these stones to become loaves of bread," Jesus countered with the truth: "No! The Scriptures say, 'People do not live by bread alone, but by every word that comes from the mouth of God.'" Learn your battling strategies from the Master Sword-handler.

5. Pray for others who are going through similar circumstances: pray for a loved one's salvation, pray for missionaries in the world, pray for your neighbors to come to God. Use Satan's attack on you as a reminder to pray for others. By doing this, you are getting out of yourself, shifting your focus from you to others in need. Instead of giving Satan his desired response, you are answering it with prayer.

Let's look at a scenario from earlier in the book as an example. Your pastor asked you to lead a Bible study at church. You prayed about it and felt led to do it. That is when the attack happened, and the old harmful responses came welling up in your recipe of failure:

- Who do you think you are to lead a Bible study? You're not smart enough.
- God can't use you.
- If others knew about your past, they wouldn't have anything to do with you.
- No one will come.
- It's going to fail. *You're* going to fail!

But if you are to rewrite this recipe with healthy ingredients, this is how your new recipe might look:

- If God called me to lead this Bible study, He will equip me!
- God can use anyone willing to serve Him.
- God can use me despite my past; my past does not dictate my future.
- God will bring the people to the study He wants to be there—I will choose to trust Him.
- If God has ordained this Bible study, and I allow Him to work, it will not fail.
- This Bible study is all about God, not me.
- I will focus on and pray for others who are teaching.

Meditate on His truth daily, if not more, reflecting on who God is and who you are in Christ. Every time doubt starts knocking at the door, choose to answer it with the truth. With this new recipe, you will serve with a good measure of enthusiasm.

We tend to move in the direction we are focused on. When we focus on the lies we tell ourselves, we receive the by-products of those lies. The same holds true when we focus on the truth. We end up moving toward and receiving the by-products of the truth. We are always focused on something...why not focus on the truth and reap the rewards?

Achilles Heel

To be effective in your offensive battle, you will need to identify what your Achilles heel is. Your self-worth, finances, your family, your past...whatever it is, the Achilles heel is like an emotional nerve. Every time it's hit, you feel the pain while your blood pressure hits the roof. It may even tie knots in your stomach and cause you to lose sleep.

Once you've identified your Achilles heel, you will need to figure out when you are most prone to attack. I am a morning person, and that is when I am at my best. However, as soon as the clock strikes ten at night (my wife, the night owl, argues that it's nine), I go brain-dead. That is when my energy level is running on empty, and I find myself getting a little snippy. I am also more prone to spiritual attack during this time of day. An ingredient I use during this time is a journal. I write about my day and spend a few moments in God's Word. I know this is not the time to get into any heavy discussions or any major problem-solving.

By recognizing my Achilles heel and when I'm at my best and when I'm at my weakest, I avoid setting myself up for frustration and attacks. I am more prepared, more aware, and able to be more proactive.

Take a minute to pray and ask God what your Achilles heel is. What is the one thing Satan uses the most in your life to attack you? What throws you into a downward spiral, negative thinking, guilt, or shame? Ask God to reveal this to you and write it below.

My Achilles heel: _____

Take another minute to pray and think about the time of day you are most vulnerable to Satan's attacks. Is it at one in the morning when your chest clenches with the guilt, shame, sinful thoughts, or fears? Is it before an important business meeting or presentation? Or does it greet you the moment your alarm startles you awake? It could be these or any number of times in your day. When is the most prevalent time Satan attacks you with swirling thoughts?

When I am most prone to attack: _____

Now that you know how and when Satan attacks you most, you can pray and ask God to show you how to create your offense. How will you take your thoughts captive and stop them? What thoughts will you use to challenge the attack? What truth from God's Word will you take out to fight with? Who will you pray for to move your focus to others?

My offensive strategy: _____

_____

_____

_____

_____

_____

Now you will be ready for Satan next time he shows up.

In the Moment

I bought a cheap watch from a crazy man
floating down a canal.
It doesn't use numbers or moving hands
it always just says now.
Now you may be thinking that I was had,
but this watch is never wrong
and if I have trouble the warranty said,
breathe in, breathe out, move on.
—Jimmy Buffett

So much of what creates emotional, spiritual, and relational turmoil is the inability to spend most of our time in the here and now. Have you ever been talking with someone, looking right at them, but your mind is running through the list of unfinished tasks at home or the office? Or your thoughts are drifting back to something that happened earlier in the day? You see their mouth moving, but you're not hearing a word they're saying. We can be with someone, but not be with them. When this happens, we miss out on what is happening in the present. We can do this in other areas of our lives as well. We get so caught up in rushing around that we miss out on a lot of what God has for us in the here and now.

One year when the kids were young, our family went hiking at Mammoth Cave National Park. Being the impatient personality that I am, I had calculated the pace we would need to travel in order to be back for lunch, and it was a pretty steady pace. It not only would get us back in time for lunch, but possibly home in time for me to get some work done (even though it was my day off). We started our three-mile hike around nine that morning. We had no more gotten started when one of the kids stopped by some boulders and asked to climb on them. I told them no, we needed to keep moving.

A few minutes later, one of them said, "Daddy, what kind of tree is this?"

I said, "I don't know. We've gotta keep moving if we're gonna get back by lunch."

"Daddy, look at those bugs! What kind of bugs are they, Daddy? I think I'll name that bug Bob!"

I responded, "Kids, why are you dragging your feet? Don't you want to get back for lunch? If you do, you need to stop wasting time!"

My son looked up at me and said, "No, Daddy, we just want to be with you and Mommy!"

My family had the right frame of mind. They wanted to enjoy what they were doing at that moment. They were enjoying just *being*. Not me! I had an agenda! All I wanted was to get back for lunch. I was somewhere off in the future, so much so that any delay in MY plan created frustration in me. I made it known to the others that I was upset through my tone, rolling my eyes, and my overall impatience. Ephesians 5:15-16 says, "Be very careful, then, how you live—not as unwise but as wise, making the most of every opportunity, because the days are evil." This verse says to make the most out of every opportunity, not every opportunity hoped for. The human race was designed by God to move at camel speed, but we are trying to live at light speed! We need to relearn the art of being still and adding the ingredient of living in the moment to our recipe.

CHAPTER ELEVEN
The Conscience Ingredient

The first rule is to keep an untroubled spirit. The second is to look things in the face and know them for what they are.

—Marcus Aurelius

I strive always to keep my conscience clear before God and man.

Acts 24:16

When my son Erik was around three years old, it was my turn to put him to bed while Kathy lay down with our daughter Emily. Erik was having a hard time falling asleep, so I snuggled up with him, his head lying on my chest. I decided to sing to him, thinking that would help him go to sleep. Bad idea! Anyone who has heard me sing will tell you I can't sing. I try to bellow out a tune, but even at church when I open my mouth to sing, I get some interesting looks. My repertoire of songs is limited, and the only one I could think of at that moment was the old song, "Down in the Valley."

I started singing, "Down in the valley, the valley so low, hang your head over, hear the wind blow. Hear the winds blow dear, hear the wind blow." Erik went from not being sleepy to being depressed listening to the lyrics of the song. I continued to sing, and soon

I felt his little hand tapping me on my chest. Then he said in his sweet little voice, "Daddy, Mom said, 'Stop singing!'" You know you're a bad singer if even your three-year-old is telling you to stop singing! He then giggled to himself and fell asleep.

There are times in our lives when we must get honest with the way things are turning out for us. Irwin Edman wrote: "Life is always at some turning point."[39] That turning point is when we get honest with some of the problems we are facing, knowing that we are the cause—not the victim— of the troubles that are happening to us, our relationships, or life in general.

In chapter five, we learned about the dangers of sin and temptation. In this chapter, we will look at the effect sin has on our life recipes and the importance of fighting it.

Proverbs 28:13 says, "People who conceal their sins will not prosper, but if they confess and turn from them they will receive mercy" (NLT). If it is our goal to have a healthy, successful life, we have to deal with the issue of sin and how it can spoil our recipe. Living in disobedience can destroy any recipe, and our concealed sin will keep us from prospering. That is why this next section is so important in rewriting our recipe. It's the foundation to the other ingredients.

Humble yourselves under the mighty hand of God, that He may exalt you in due time, casting all your cares upon Him, for He cares for you. (1 Peter 5:6-7 NKJV)

In this passage, Peter gives some keen insight pertaining to the stress and worries we experience in our lives. He cites that obedience is a stress reducer. Peter reasons there can be no peace and we will not experience a healthy life recipe outside of God's moral and ethical guidelines. The more we actively choose to live

---

[39] https://www.brainyquote.com/quotes/irwin_edman_127619

outside of God's protective boundaries, the more we will experience a deepening sense of frustration, fear, unrest, and anxiety.

> You have laid down precepts that are to be fully obeyed. Oh, that my ways were steadfast in obeying your decrees. Then I would not be put to shame when I consider all your commands. I will praise you with an upright heart as I learn your righteous laws. I will obey your decrees; do not utterly forsake me. (Psalm 119:4-8)

It is not that we are ignorant of God's boundaries for us. More times than not, we know the right thing to do, but we choose to go counter to it. Then, because of our disobedience, we have to endure the painful consequences of doing our own thing. Too many times we think we know what is best for us and so we put conditions on God's Word:

"Yes, I know God said not to do this in His Word . . . but times were different back then!"

"God's Word is just giving you options . . . if we want to follow them, great, if not, that is fine too."

In essence, we remove God from the throne, and we seat ourselves in that place of honor, wisdom, and authority. We become the god of our own life. Satan did the same thing. Ever since his fall from heaven, he has been twisting God's Word to suit his own purposes. He chooses to walk outside of God's commands, willfully disobeying.

> How you have fallen from heaven, morning star, son of the dawn! You have been cast down to the earth, you, who once laid low the nations! You said in your heart, "I will ascend to heaven; I will raise my

throne above the stars of God; I will sit enthroned on the mount of assembly, on the utmost heights of the sacred mountain. I will ascend above the tops of the clouds, I will make myself like the Most High." (Isaiah 14:12-14)

Satan knows God. He knows God's Word. In fact, he knows it even better than we do. Yet he still chose to go his own way and do his own thing.

According to A.W. Tozer, "We, in our disobedience, are walking dangerously parallel to Satan."[40] Psalm 119:59-60 says, "I have considered my ways and have turned my steps to your statues. I will hasten and not delay to obey your commands." Living obediently removes layers of potential stress caused by disobedient life choices we make.

Much of the stress we experience is the direct result of sin, whether our own or someone else's. In his book, "The Pursuit of God," Tozer states that all our heartaches and a great many of our physical ills spring directly from our sins. Pride, arrogance, resentfulness, evil imaginings, malice, and greed are sources of more human pain than all of the diseases that ever afflicted mortal flesh.[41]

Disobedience compounds stress. In the marital relationship, for instance, when a husband does not love his wife as Christ loved the church and a wife does not treat her husband with respect, stress fills the home. When children do not obey their parents, or when parents fail to train up a child in a God-honoring manner, implementing scriptural principles of discipline and love, stress fills the home. When laws are broken, stress engulfs the offender

---

[40] A.W. Tozer, *The Pursuit of God*, (Kindle Edition)
[41] Ibid.

as they worry about getting caught. A person who has cheated on his taxes is filled with anxiety and stress as he anticipates being called in for an audit. The one who broke trust with a friend or a loved one by being deceitful is dreading being caught in their lie.

We all have something inside us of our own making that has the capability to either grant us peace or cause inner turmoil—an ingredient that promotes either soul rest or soul distress. The ingredient is a good or bad conscience. An untroubled conscience is the most important heart condition we can have if we want to recapture joy in our lives.

Joy comes through the feeling of peace: peace with ourselves and peace with the way we have responded to family members, friends, and with God. Second Corinthians 1:12 says, "Now this is our boast: Our conscience testifies that we have conducted ourselves in the world, and especially in our relations with you, with integrity and godly sincerity. We have done so, relying not on worldly wisdom but on God's grace." A French proverb says, "There is no pillow so soft as a clear conscience." What a tremendous witness it is to have a good conscience that brings peace and satisfaction into a person's heart.

Can you remember a time as a child when you knowingly and willfully disobeyed your parents—a time when you did the total opposite of what you should have done? I know I do. When I was sixteen, my folks were going out of town for a few days, and it was going to be the first time I was allowed to stay home alone without adult supervision. Big mistake!

My parents left a list of "to-dos" and "not-to-dos." One item that was on the "not-to-do"' list was not to even think about driving the car anywhere without them with me. I did pretty well with the list for the first four minutes, but then I had the great idea to take the car (that I was not supposed to drive) and go pick up a good friend of mine to go riding around the back roads. Major mistake!

Even while I was putting the key into the ignition, a little voice in the back of my head told me that this was not a good idea and that I should turn off the car and go back into the house. But, like so many of us do, I ignored it and off I went. I picked up my friend and started driving up and down the back roads. It had rained the night before, so there were all these wonderful water puddles to drive through, and I guarantee you that we hit every single one of them as we drove back-and-forth on those graveled backroads. The longer we drove and the louder our laughter got, the quieter that little voice became in my mind.

Just before it was time to drop off my friend at his house, we thought we would make one more pass down a straightaway with a lot of big water puddles. Major, major mistake!

Seeing that this was going to be the last time we went down that road, I decided to go little faster, to hit those water puddles a little harder, to make a bigger splash. We were getting closer to the end of the straightaway and to a steel guard rail that would force us to either make a sharp left or a sharp right to avoid hitting it.

After we went through the last water puddle, I started to press the brakes so we could make the turn, but unbeknownst to me, water had gotten into the brake pads, which meant—we had no brakes!

It is truly amazing that hysterical laughter can turn to silence all in the moment of a single heartbeat. I looked over at my friend. When he realized that we weren't going to stop and that we were going to hit the guard rail, his face mirrored my panic and horror. In that split-second when we made impact with the guard rail, everything slowed down. That was when the little voice showed up again, reminding me that disobeying my parents and taking the car was a bad idea. But thanks to God, my friend only ended up with a few bruises and I with a few stitches in my leg. The scar on my leg still reminds me today of the importance of listening to that little voice.

Do you remember doing something like this? Some large or

small act of disobedience? Something your parents told you not to do? You may have even lied about it when confronted by your parents. Do you remember how paranoid you felt and the fear you felt when the "what ifs" came visiting your thoughts? Do you remember how it robbed you of your joy?

What if they find out?

What if someone saw me?

What if they tell on me?

What if I get punished?

What if? What if? What if?

Webster says *conscience* is "the sense of what is right or wrong in one's conduct or motives, impelling one toward right action."[42] Even though our conscience can cause us pain, it is a necessary component that makes us human. Without it, men would be devoid of that faculty that brings his greatest joy—his own approval. Without conscience, man would not be man.

If we do what we think is the right thing, our conscience approves us and, in doing so, gives us a feeling of self-respect and peace. But if we knowingly do wrong (as we so often do), there is an internal witness that blames and torments us. When we do what is right, it harmonizes and unifies us on the inside, but doing what is wrong causes disconnection and frustration. A guilty conscience causes unrest and inner turbulence.

Daniel Webster said, "There is no evil we cannot face or flee from but the consequences of duty disregarded. A sense of obligation pursues us ever. It is omnipresent like the Deity. If we take to ourselves wings of the morning and dwell in the uttermost parts of the sea, duty performed or duty violated is still with us, for our happiness or our misery."[43]

---

[42] https://www.merriam-webster.com/dictionary/conscience

[43] https://www.goodreads.com/quotes/search?utf8=%E2%9C%93&q=daniel+webster&commit=Search

A conscience infected with guilt from our past wrongs can make cowards and defeatists of us all. It is like a millstone tied around our neck, pulling us downward. It warps our perception, causing us to always be on the defensive, often afraid of our own shadow. As we try to hide what we have done, we end up dragging the millstone around with us.

We are like the man traveling in a wagon who asked a passerby, "How much more of this hill is there?" The passerby responded, "Hill? There's no hill. Man, your hind wheels are off!"

Traveling with the ingredient of a nagging and painful conscience is like walking continuously uphill. It wears us down and we become exhausted from all the energy we expend trying to keep our thoughts locked away.

Studies have proven that a disturbed conscience creates stress. That stress can make us sick by hindering our immune system from operating the way it should in fighting off infection. If we are harboring any unrepented sin, it's hard for us to have any emotional rest when we are being convicted. A sick, disconnected conscience can make a person ill emotionally, physically, and spiritually.

The Over-Stimulated Conscience

Our conscience can also become *over*-stimulated, out of balance, functioning beyond the purpose for which it was intended. You see, our conscience, or inner voice, acts as a warning system. It warns us, hopefully, before we commit a wrong. It cries out, convicting us of our offense. If we do wrong, it is the necessary duty of conscience to condemn and indict us. But when we repent and God's forgiveness has been granted, our conscience should be clear.

First John 1:9 says, "If we confess our sins, he is faithful and just and will forgive us our sins and purify us from all unrighteousness." When we repent and confess our sins to God, according to

Scripture, God's forgiveness should take the hammer of judgment from our conscience and give us peace.

Once our conscience has accomplished its task and we have changed, there is nothing to be gained by tormenting us anymore. If it does, it then ceases to be an asset and becomes a detriment. The haunting of yesterday's sin is dispersed by God's grace. However, when we mentally resurrect it, it hangs over us like a storm cloud. Our reluctance to forgive ourselves keeps our lives in bondage.

Not forgiving ourselves, even though God has already done so, puts us in the position of assuming the role of God in our life. If God forgives us when we ask for His forgiveness, (and He does), and if He says He remembers our sins no more, (and He doesn't), then who are we to try to hold on to it? And what benefit is it to us?

If a hurting conscience is not dealt with, it will become infected and fester. It will not only cause the possessor to become worse, but may also become a powerful force in hurting others. Those with an infected conscience may project themselves by accusing others of the mistakes they themselves have committed. The liar feels justified denouncing lying in others; the gossip's conscience feels cleaner by trying to find some fault in others; the thief feels upright by condemning others who steal. Doing this, we take the focus off our own sin and project it on others. When we do this, we end up rationalizing our own sin, while condemning what others are doing.

We need to be careful if we find ourselves demonstrating this behavior; it is shaky ground to walk on. Romans 2:1 says, "You, therefore, have no excuse, you who pass judgment on someone else, for at whatever point you judge another, you are condemning yourself, because you who pass judgment do the same things."

Before I bought the car I now drive, I hardly ever saw the same make out on the street, so I thought no one else had the one I wanted. However, as soon as I drove the car out of the dealership,

I began to see that everybody and their mother was driving the same car. Prior to buying my car, I had hardly seen it on the road, but now that I owned it, I couldn't go anywhere without seeing someone driving it around.

The same concept pertains to our sins. We notice most clearly the sin in others that often has taken root in our own lives. If we dare do a self-evaluation, we may find that we are committing the same sin. It might be in a more socially acceptable form, but it's the same sin.

I am not saying we are not to speak out against sin, but when we do so, it must be done in a spirit of humility. Before I confront others, I need to check myself out as well. In Psalm 139:23-24, David cries out to God, "Search me, O God and know my heart; test me and know my anxious thoughts. See if there is any offensive way in me, and lead me in the way everlasting." In my own life, when I have prayed to God to deal with or change someone I am having a problem with, it seems like I am the one He ends up changing.

Matthew 7:3-5 admonishes us, "Why do you look at the speck of sawdust in your brother's eye and pay no attention to the plank in your own eye? How can you say to your brother, 'Let me take the speck out of your eye,' when all the time there is a plank in your own eye? You hypocrite, first take the plank out of your own eye,   and then you will see clearly to remove the speck from your brother's eye."

A conscience at peace is such an essential part of living a good life that the Scriptures include it in the summation of God's commandment to us: "The goal of this command is love, which comes from a pure heart and a good conscience and a sincere faith" (1 Timothy 1:5).

By having a good conscience and a heart at peace, we are able to have more confidence in God. It is also the catalyst for your healthy life recipe.

CHAPTER TWELVE

Your Best Recipe

Of all the paths a man could strike into,
there is, at any given moment, a best path . . .
a thing which, here and now, it were of all things
wisest for him to do . . . to find this path,
and walk in it, is the one thing needful for him.
—Thomas Carlyle

All of us cooks have a recipe that we have perfected over many years. We like to serve it to guests when they come over for dinner. Our families love this recipe and ask for it on a regular basis. When someone takes that first bite, they know it was made with love. To make a dish with love means you are taking special care to make sure it turns out perfectly. This could mean cutting the fat off a piece of meat, mixing in the flour carefully so there are no lumps in the gravy, or taking the time to julienne a carrot just right to get the perfect amount of crunch.

We can work on our life recipe in much the same way. We can take time to change our thought patterns from harsh to loving, from negative to joyful, from sinful to victorious. We can treasure God's Word in our hearts so our reactions, behaviors, and words will be what God wants from us. In changing our recipes, we will change our relationships for the better and live more peaceful, joyful lives. And truly, "A good man brings good things out of the good stored up in him" (Matthew 12:35).

Let's look at this example of a healthy recipe to get an idea of some of the ingredients you can add to your recipe to live a more joyful, productive, and significant life.

A Recipe for Healthy Living

- Make time for daily quiet time with God to align your priorities with Him.
- Uncrowd your schedule and allow time to think and act spontaneously.
- Exercise your "no" muscle—define and defend your boundaries.
- Stop and smell the roses—or enjoy the sunset, or time with your kids—make the most of each opportunity.
- Be kind to yourself—in your actions and thoughts.
- Be kind to others—in your actions and words.
- Choose your battles.
- Stop judging, assuming, catastrophizing, etc.
- Don't worry, pray instead—there's no benefit from worrying, but tremendous benefit from prayer.
- Don't take yourself so seriously—learn to laugh.
- Make time to connect with others.

The 60/30/10 Mixture—Live in the Moment

Someone once said, "If we spend our time with regrets over yesterday, and worries over what might happen tomorrow, we have no today in which to live."[44]

---

[44] Author unknown.

Approximately 60 percent of our thoughts are about the future. They might be, "What's going to happen when . . . ?" "What if . . . ?" "Once I get to . . ." I could have had a great weekend, but when five o'clock on Sunday comes along, I start dreading Monday, which robs me of the rest of Sunday! In fact, the more I focus on the future, the more anxious I become. Most of what I worry about, I have no control over, which makes me worry more.[45] Matthew 6:34 tells us, "Do not worry about tomorrow, for tomorrow will worry about itself. Each day has enough trouble of its own."

Approximately 30 percent of our thoughts are focused on the past—regrets, missed opportunities, "Why did I . . . ?" and "should've, could've, would've," statements. It's a vicious cycle—the more I replay the past event, the more depressed I become.

That leaves only 10 percent for the here and now. Only 10 percent of the time are we are fully in the present. This is not a very big number! If I were going to have surgery and only had a 10 percent chance of success, I probably wouldn't have surgery! If my marriage had only a 10 percent chance of success, I probably wouldn't get married! If I only gave my family 10 percent of my time, I wouldn't have very close relationships. Ten percent just isn't enough in order to achieve success in any area of our lives.

Most of us have experienced living in the moment. They are the moments when we are listening to our favorite song, when we are caught up in a movie or play, when we are hanging on every word of a gifted speaker, when our child was born, or when our child is experiencing something the first time and we can re-experience it through their eyes.

Living in the moment means that we give our full attention to

---

[45] Living in the moment does not mean that we shouldn't plan for the future. It is a very different thing to plan for the future than to be anxious or worried about the future. Part of being a responsible steward is to prepare for the future. When we are prepared, we are less likely to worry.

the moment. If we are playing with our children, we need to block out all distractions and play with our children. If we are having a conversation with a friend or our spouse, we need to block out all distractions and give them our full attention. Think of how many blessings and opportunities we miss out on because our attention is focused on the past or future! If we begin to incorporate the ingredient of living in the moment, think of how many blessings and opportunities we will experience!

> *According to my watch the time is now*
> *Past is dead and gone*
> *Don't try to shake it just nod your head*
> *Breathe In, Breathe Out, Move on*
> *Don't try to shake it just bow your head*
> *Breathe in, Breathe out, Move on.*
> —Jimmy Buffett

Being Proactive

Very often, we seem to take the victim's role in our circumstances. We don't need to let our circumstance drive us, our emotions, or who we are. We need to have a picture in our mind of the way we want to behave or react to circumstances. This will help guide us when we face any difficulty or unexpected turns in the road.

Our daughter had been riding horses for four years and was pretty good at it! She had several awesome instructors who influenced her positively. Prior to these instructors, she had an instructor who was a yeller, and she also had a friend at the barn who had passed some negative habits on to her. She was now riding a young horse, finding herself easily frustrated, and exhibiting some of these bad habits she'd picked up along the way.

I had noticed and was talking to her about this one night. She said, "I just don't know what to do!" I told her to get a picture in her mind of how she wants to be able to act the next time she gets frustrated—does she want to get angry and take it out on the horse? Or does she want to stay calm and positive and teach the horse what he needs to do? Of course, she chose the latter scenario. If she knows ahead of time that she wants to be a calm and positive presence, most likely that mindset will guide her toward her desired outcome. It is so important for us to be proactive and take an active role in our own lives—instead of letting life happen to us, dictated by circumstance, we can take charge and cause things to happen. Stop being a victim! Have a plan and make it happen!

When Healthy Recipes Fail

My mother-in-law makes the best chocolate meringue pie! She has followed the same recipe for years. However, sometimes the meringue "weeps." This weeping has nothing to do with following the recipe. It has more to do with outside circumstances, such as humidity. This is something over which she has no control. The same thing can happen to us in our lives.

Look at Jehoshaphat in 2 Chronicles 19-20. He did everything God told him to do. He tore down the asher poles, he appointed judges, he was a godly man. God was at the center of his recipe. However, he got word that the "ites" (Moabites, Ammonites, and Meunites) were out to get him. He didn't run, he didn't doubt God, he didn't doubt his calling. He sought God first, and then he thanked God for His promises. He was honest with God, declaring his dependency on Him.

That's when God spoke to him through the prophet, Jahaziel, and said, "Do not be afraid or discouraged because of this vast army. For the battle is not yours, but God's. . . . You will not have to fight this battle. Take up your positions; stand firm and see the

151

deliverance the LORD will give you. . . . Do not be afraid; do not be discouraged. Go out to face them tomorrow, and the LORD will be with you" (2 Chronicles 20:15,17).

We all have "ites" that are after us, even when we're following the recipe. Sometimes life doesn't cooperate, sometimes children make poor choices, and sometimes God is trying to grow us. We have gone through the process of identifying harmful ingredients, removing them and replacing them with healthy ingredients, being mindful of what we're passing down to our children, and rewriting our life's recipes. We can follow the new recipe step-by-step, consistently over time, and yet the outcome is just not what it should be.

When our recipe doesn't turn out how it should, the story of Jehoshaphat shows us the core ingredients we need to lean on. (1) Trust God that He has written our life's recipe and that He will sustain us. (2) Know that God is sovereign and that whatever we are going through in life at any given time does not surprise Him. He saw it coming long before we did. And (3), because of His sovereignty, He not only knows what difficulties we are facing in life, but He has already made provisions to deal with them. "'For I know the plans I have for you,' declares the Lord, 'plans to prosper you and not to harm you, plans *to give you hope and a future*'" (Jeremiah 29:11 emphasis added).

Mixing in the Right Ingredients

I love going to my in-laws for dinner! My mother-in-law is an incredible cook, and by the time I push myself away from the dinner table, I feel fifty pounds heavier!

I enjoy the family atmosphere, catching up on everybody's lives, and while we are talking, we are passing the food around the table. For the most part I am not a picky eater, and I'll take what is passed to me if I like it. However, there are a couple items that I will quickly pass on: brussels sprouts and grits. The brussels sprouts because of their smell, and the grits because I am not even sure what a grit is, and I don't want anything to do with it! Everything else gets heaped onto my plate.

It is a wonderful thing when we have good foods to eat and pass on the foods we don't like. We can also think of our thoughts in the same way. There are thoughts that produce helpful fruit and contribute to our lives. Those are the ones that we want to hang onto, spend time with and feed on. The other thoughts that come across our plates are those that makes us feel sicker and sicker the longer we have them in front of us, and our anxiety levels rise. Those are the ones we want to pass as quickly as we can to the one who is sitting next to us—Jesus.

Jesus tells me through His Word that I'm to cast all my cares upon Him, turn over all those points of worry, and then receive His peace that surpasses all understanding.

This is good news! We can let go of the thoughts that create anxieties, fears, sins, and any negativity that brings us down and pick up those thoughts that promote peace, joy, and a sense of well-being. This means we have to be purposeful in our selections. We choose which ones to keep and which ones to pass off.

Sometimes we will accept things we really don't want out of habit ("I have been this way for years"). We buy into the lie that we're just stuck with it and that we don't have a choice ("I can't change"). The truth is, we can be pickier about what we allow in our thought lives and Scripture backs that truth up!

When mixing up your life's recipe, you need to have the right ingredients and replace the bad ingredients. Take a minute to read through the list of ingredients below. Next to each bad ingredient is a good ingredient that counters it. These are some suggested ingredients and is not an exhaustive list by any means. I have left several empty slots at the bottom so you can write in those good and bad ingredients that are true to your life. As you go through this list, look for bad ingredients you need to replace and good ingredients you need to add. Circle the ingredients you want to lose and put a line through them. Place a check mark by the good ingredients you already have. And place a star by the ones you want God to help you add to your life recipe. Be sure to write into the blanks any other ingredients you may have or want that aren't listed here.

Bad Ingredients	Good Ingredients
Blame-shifting	Lose interest in finding fault
Catastrophizing	Keep things in perspective
Can't-stand-its	Respond graciously to annoyances
What-ifs	Stay grounded in reality, not fantasy
Assuming	Separate fact from fiction
Shoulds and musts	Ask God what he really wants of me and others
All-or-nothing	Do my best and leave the rest in God's hands
Comparing	Live in constant thankfulness
Perfectionism	Let myself and others be human
Labeling	Be kind to myself and others
Sinful thoughts	Use the Word of God as a sword

Bad Ingredients	Good Ingredients

Now write your good life recipe below using the good ingredients you starred and checked. Use the tools in this book to help rid yourself of the bad ingredients you circled.

My Life Recipe

Ingredients:

- _____
- _____
- _____
- _____
- _____
- _____
- _____
- _____
- _____
- _____
- _____

Directions: _____

_____

_____

_____

_____

_____

A Final Thought

Romans 12:2 states that we are no longer to be conformed to this world but are to be transformed by the renewing of our mind. So, according Scripture, to be transformed we must work on renewing our mindset. Another way to say this is that we need to actively change the way we think about ourselves, others, and the situations we face. When we start to realign our thoughts to reflect who God says we are in Jesus, how He says we are to view others, and how He says to live life, we will start living in freedom. "You will know the truth, and the truth will set you free" (John 8:32).

Renewing your mind is not just about positive or Pollyanna thinking. It's about clinging to the truth while letting go of the deceptions of the enemy. It's not only about hearing what God is telling us through His Word but about embracing it as truth—instead of the old lies that we have been buying into.

So many of God's children are living shackled to the past, to a distorted sense of self, and to negative perspectives of others and their future. What would our lives look like if we were no longer enslaved to the toxic lies that so often keep us stuck in harmful patterns? Could you imagine what could be accomplished if God's children were set free?

One of Satan's techniques to keep us stuck is to convince us to believe that we don't have what we already own—our freedom, our victory, and even our new identity. The questions we have to ask ourselves are: Who do I believe is telling me the truth, and who do I believe has my best interest at heart?

> Today I have given you the choice between life and death, between blessings and curses. Now I call on heaven and earth to witness the choice you make.

> Oh, that you would choose life, so that you and your
> descendants might live! (Deuteronomy 30:19 NLT)

It takes work to change our habitual thinking patterns. It's easier to go the route of least resistance and continue to allow those unhealthy thoughts to dominate and contaminate our lives, that's the easier path to take. But if we really want to experience the freedom that God wants us to have, we need to live more intentionally and take control of our thoughts. We must choose to align ourselves with God's truth more than we want to align ourselves with the lies of the enemy. When we choose good ingredients in our life recipes— the things of God—it will change our behaviors, our relationships, and our walks with God.

I pray that God will bless you as you move forward in His Spirit. When you have the Holy Spirit on your side, He will help you in your transformation. Ask Him to bless your work as you change your life recipe, and ask Him to sculpt and shape your heart along the way to be more like Jesus.

About the Author

Rick is a certified Christian marriage and family therapist and a certified cognitive behavioral therapist. He received his B.A from Morningside College and an M.A. and D. Min from Central Christian University. He has worked in the mental health field for the past thirty-four years—eleven and a half years in inpatient psychiatric hospitals and the remainder in his private practice in Bowling Green, KY.

"Rethink is a product of my years working as a therapist and also from my own life struggles. My passion is to help set people free from the bondages that are keeping them stuck in self-destructive patterns."

CPSIA information can be obtained
at www.ICGtesting.com
Printed in the USA
BVHW032113071119
563174BV00018B/16/P